THANKS:

To my wife Cristina, my sons Ricardo and Miguel and my sister Dulce, for their support in all moments of my career.

To my parents for the education that they provide me, preparing me to live in a world in constant change.

To all my colleagues from 18 countries that shared their networking stories.

To Clare and Ólisteph for their support and revision.

To Edições Sílabo, with a special word to my editor Manuel Robalo that believed in me from the begining.

NETWORKING

Your Professional
Survival Guide

FILIPE CARRERA

EDIÇÕES SÍLABO

Sílabo can be visited in:

www.silabo.pt

Editor: Manuel Robalo

FICHA TÉCNICA:

Title: Networking – Your Professional Survival Guide
Author: Filipe Carrera
© Edições Sílabo, Lda.
Cover: Pedro Mota

1st Edition
Lisbon, 2010.
Printing: Rolo & Filhos II, S.A.
DL: 311944/10
ISBN: 978-972-618-586-4

EDIÇÕES SÍLABO, LDA.

R. Cidade de Manchester, 2
1170-100 LISBOA
Telf.: 218130345
Fax: 218166719
e-mail: silabo@silabo.pt
www.silabo.pt

Table of Contents

Chapter 2

NETWORKING OPPORTUNITIES

Chapter 3

YOUR PRESENTATION

Chapter 4

KNOWLEDGE NETWORKS

Chapter 5

NETWORK PRESENCE

Chapter 6

THE POWER OF SOCIAL MEDIA

Chapter 7

WORKING ON THE NET

Chapter 8

THE NETWORKER TALKS

Chapter 9

SIMPLIFICATION

Preface

Filipe Carrera surprises us in this book Networking – Professional Survival Guide, even after having recently released the bestseller Digital Marketing in the Version 2.0.

In his first book, after referring to structural changes currently taking place in consumers' behavior and the business modus operandi, he teaches the reader how to use, in practice, digital media (the Internet, mobile phones, etc.) to generate and develop businesses.

From that point on, Filipe Carrera promotes a digital community as a dynamic space that allows for an interaction between the author and his readers. In other words, he applies one of the sides of networking, the subject of his new book.

Networking, for the contacts it provides, is a unique unattainable value for our personal and professional life.

Throughout the years, we build our contact network, which includes family members, friends, school and work colleagues, although, in our mind, we don't have this structuring concept of networking or a network.

Today, the so-called social networks are very popular, but they were always there. The development of the Internet and of the new information technologies allowed for the explosion of organized communication networks.

The network is responsible for the sharing of ideas and values among people who share common interests and goals.

Personally and professionally, a good contact network will make your life easier and will create value. Nevertheless, only relatively few recognize the capabilities and potentials at their disposal online, the gain of being integrated into selected networks for their professional life.

The organized construction of a contact network is not born out of spontaneous generation. It has to be carefully generated and nurtured with professionalism over time. Filipe Carrera teaches us, throughout the book's several chapters, how to generate networking opportunities, how to create knowledge networks, how to be and work within them and how to develop them, in order to optimize the effort (investment) that is thus being made.

Today, the permanent bond we have with the world that surrounds us is a condition necessary even for survival; in the country we live in, in the social communities we enjoy and in the professional industries that we are connected to, both nationally and internationally.

Hence the meaning of the title's second part: Networking – Your Professional Survival Guide, Filipe Carrera is not exaggerating. No matter how competent one is on an individual level, whoever acts isolated and not within a network, does not have much chance of success in the competitive and ever-more globalized world we live in.

Primary networks of relationships between individuals originate quasi-groups. These are formed by all the relations established by people in their everyday life and may be composed of friends, work colleagues, university colleagues, military service colleagues, family members, neighbors, organizations, etc.

These are the relationship networks that are started during our childhood and that contribute towards the formation of identities.

On the other hand, secondary and intermediary networks are formed by the collectiveness, by the institutions or by the people that share a common interest, people that might achieve a greater success if their efforts were jointly mobilized and there is an organized articulation.

The reader, through Filipe Carrera's book, will be awakened to the importance of networking, both in primary relationships as in secondary and intermediary relationships. In short, awakened to a tool that might be helpful in a diversity of tasks: for instance, promotion of skills, job opportunities, business proposals, selection of experts, meeting old friends and colleagues, etc...

Social and business networking in the digital era is a world to be explored, but in an organized and coherent way towards defined goals.

I advise the reader to enter networking through the educational way used by Filipe Carrera in this book, where he uses his global experiences in Consulting, Training and Coaching to explain the networking advantages and paths, linking it to the countries' level of development. Filipe Carrera uses a very simple and practical language which will surely appeal to readers.

October 2009
Eduardo Catroga
Former Minister of Finance, Portugal

Introduction

In the world we live in, it is not enough to be competent, dynamic, pro-active, knowledgeable, assertive, determined... or any other epithets that will look fantastic in any given CV. It is absolutely necessary that the market and the people recognize the qualities in a person, both as a human being and as a professional.

We might even question: Could there be an excellent professional, if the market or the people fail to recognize him/her as such?

The reason why networking is a part of today's agenda is not a mere coincidence; never before was there so much talk about the management of contact networks. There are networks, professionals who manage their contact network well (networkers), networking events, etc...

The crisis we are currently experiencing has made us realize that the work market is volatile, that is, we might have achieved a dream position as far as our career goes, but the following month, we might be forced to look for other alternatives in life, without even having had the time to realize how we came to this.

Networking is thus a good lifesaver, when it really should be something natural and completely a part of the life of any professional.

Moreover, networking was always present in our lives, ever since pre-historic periods, when small human communities would combine hunts, managing their contact network.

One of the greatest differences between the century we live in and the previous centuries is that, for the first time in the history of Mankind, we are not bound to our geographical space. Due to the colossal advance of information and communication technologies, we can now find experts, wherever they are, and be recognized as experts in locations very remote from our daily life.

Locations that we never visited or thought of visiting. We live in a small global village.

With this book, I wanted to recommend tools and techniques to good professionals: methods that can be used immediately, capable of placing them side by side with the world's greatest.

To achieve this, I approach two themes as a whole: Traditional networking, face-to-face, and the use of information and communication technologies, to be more efficient and to achieve more with networking events as a whole.

I believe that access to technology is not sufficient. We need to know how to use it to leverage our work, our career, our companies, as well as ourselves.

To increase the efficiency of the teachings I expose, let me tell you, dear reader, that you'll be challenged throughout the book to perform certain actions, promoting the spirit of a learning community, hoping that you will share your experiences with me, so that we all might also learn.

And how can you share? Quite simply: Just look for «Networking – Guia de Sobrevivência Profissional» on Facebook, where you'll find an array of additional resources and a space to interact with me and with other readers.

I cannot finish this short introduction without first expressing my recognition for all the people, across 18 countries, who have contributed to this book sharing their experiences as networkers, demonstrating that networking is not just a fashionable word, currently raging, but rather something interesting to any professional, in any part of the world.

A final piece of advice: Experience the power of sharing with the people in your network. Be grateful to those who share with you, – and you will see your life changing beyond your expectations.

1

WHAT IS NETWORKING?

Networking: A New Trend?

In a time when books on self-help and self-development enjoy a growing popularity, it is necessary to reflect upon and to observe to what extent the fact of being successful depends on ourselves.

Background

It is my understanding that it is necessary to understand the power of the networks we are a part of – and to use that power in order to achieve our personal and professional goals.

A social network is a social structure made of individuals or organizations, which are interconnected in diverse ways and share values, ideals, financial exchanges, ideas, friendships, romantic connections, family bonds, etc, in other words: All types of exchanges.

Networking?

Strictly speaking, networking means to utilize a social network, but in this book, we'll take it further – beyond the original meaning.

When I ask the participants of my networking seminars, in various parts of the world, about the purpose of networking, I usually get answers like these:

Social Leverage?

- «To make my businesses grow».
- «To access more knowledge».
- «To have more opportunities».
- «To increase my contact network»

The common trait to these answers is: Expansion, whether professional or personal.

When I ask myself about the purpose of networking, I often use a quote by Archimedes that states the following: «Give me a lever long enough and a fulcrum on which to place it and I shall move the world.»

Nevertheless, the reader may ask: «What does this definition, taken from the world of physics, have to do with networking?» My answer is: Everything!

Archimedes states the principle of leverage, which enables you to obtain better results with lesser effort.

So, in order to accomplish that, we need two elements:
• A lever: Networking.
• A fulcrum: The networks of which we are a part.

Thus, when we are talking about networking, we are talking about a social leverage, something that might be responsible for our future personal and professional success.

Mammoth Hunting?

It is important to demystify something right from the start. Since the existence of mankind, there has been such a thing as networking. It was always an activity performed, consciously or unconsciously.

Our pre-historic ancestors already hunted mammoths, making use of their contact network, because no one could be a solitary mammoth hunter. Due to the size of the animal, hunting mammoths had to be a team effort.

Can I learn networking?

Currently, it is becoming quite clear that our success or failure depends on the competence we have and our experience in this particular area; thus, the question comes forward: Can I learn networking?

My answer is a loud and clear yes! Just as you can also learn how to drive; but if after receiving your driver's license you fail to practice, your learning will most certainly become useless.

So, my dear reader, look at the next pages and you will find a group of recommendations that you will have to put into practice, because the reading itself does not guarantee any results.

How to put networking into practice?

Networking is not an Olympic sport; it is an activity that must be interiorized, that must be a part of our life. We need to work the network every single day, keeping in mind that our network has been under construction since kindergarten.

In the next chapters we will see that there are numerous networking opportunities, that we have to take advantage of, both in the physical world and in the digital world, because constant and conscious practice is the key for success.

networking is now your Olympic sport!

You Ltd.

Have you already realized that the world has changed? That the 21st century labor market has nothing to do with the markets from the previous centuries?

The greatest difference lies in the disappearance of the concept of «employment» as we used to know it.

An employee was someone who delegated the full responsibility for the development of his career to his employer. The latter was responsible for every aspect of this resource, particularly if we were dealing with a skilled worker.

In practice, an employee waits for his employer to provide training in a specific area, so that he may perform his tasks better; otherwise, he will still perform it, but he will be less productive.

With the global increase of skilled human resources, the world has shifted and the current dilemma is that there are plenty of employees and employers that have failed to realize this, – and will thus pay a heavy toll.

Background

The best way to survive professionally today, is to look at ourselves as a company rendering services to several companies, according to the logic of an independent professional, or exclusively to a single client (our employer).

If we think like that, we will begin to create a goal of continuously satisfying our customers and constantly searching for new clients, – thus guaranteeing our future employability.

So, I'm a company now?

But, if indeed I am supposed to perform as a company, shouldn´t I also have departments? The answer is yes, at least three:
• Marketing.
• Financial.
• Training.

My organization chart

My marketing department

When we talk about personal marketing, we often only consider self-promotion, or, in more basic terms, how to hand out business cards faster than our competitors.

Our marketing department should be responsible for clearly defining our services and the aspects that differentiate us from our competitors; only then will we be able to think about the following issues:
• What can we charge for our services?
• Shall we sell our services exclusively, or not?
• How can we promote ourselves?

Hence, we must work on our personal marketing mix; that is the only way we will be able to utilize networking effectively.

My financial department

Our financial department is responsible for creating stabile conditions (do not mistake this for wealth), so that we are able to work with proper concentration and without being constantly thinking about the conditions we will face at the end of each month.

Constant focus on financial issues reduces creative capacity and, as a consequence, productivity, that in turn creates greater financial issues, which will then affect productivity in a vicious cycle.

My training department

Human resources, that fail to be up-to-date, become obsolete at an increasingly greater rate.

I clearly remember, at the end of the 1980s, when I first started college I thought: «Five more years and I will quit studying!» I was wrong! As soon as I finished my degree, I quickly realized that my student days had only just begun.

In these times, continuous training is not an ideal to be accomplished by only a few; it is a mandatory need for every professional.

Nevertheless, we need to be aware that training should not be pursued only for the sake of training. Training should be in line with the objectives we have previously defined for ourselves.

Each of the departments defined for You Ltd. should have clear and measurable goals, all converging towards one or two strategic career goals.

Having clear goals for our professional path will be the excellence basis of networking activities. If you fail to have such objectives, you will become driftwood, always dependent on circumstances.

Goals, always goals!

(3 months)

we're launching L&D Academy

don't know what outcome is

Myths about Networking

Networking is still somewhat awkward for people, who consider this activity as something almost dishonest or as some kind of business-card-throwing sport.

For these reasons, it is important to demystify some notions often associated with networking, or they may end up causing serious harm to the people holding such thoughts.

Background

In Portugal, as good Latinos, we have a fairly schizophrenic conception about networking. Let me give you an example.

You have probably witnessed this type of situation already: «If a person gets a good job, people immediately say that such happened due to his/her contacts!» But, if this happens to a competitor, a neighbor or a colleague, people immediately say: «Some strings were pulled!».

This type of attitude stops people from openly working a contact network, since they do not wish to be mistaken for mediocre people, who only make their way through life by pulling strings. Ironically, by thinking like that, we leave an open space for those who pull strings as a profession.

If we closely observe the societies in which people are more aware of the importance of networking, we find, interestingly enough, the most developed territories: USA, Japan and Northern Europe. Could this be a mere coincidence? I refuse to believe that.

Contacts and favors

It is essential to shatter this myth. It is one of the roots for some countries' lower development rates, including Portugal.

Networking is only for Job-seekers

Sometimes, while engaged in a conversation with friends, I try to
make them aware of the need to work their contact networks and
usually I'm confronted with an answer that goes something like this:
«That is very interesting, but I'm not thinking about changing jobs».

For the same reason, when these people are unemployed or want to
change jobs, they start making an approximation to networking as if it
was a transitional activity, expecting nothing short of a miracle. But, at the
end of a few days or months, they will be the first to report zero results.

Networking is an activity that goes beyond job-seeking – it adds
value to us as professionals. It opens horizons and provides access
to extraordinary opportunities.

Networking has specific moments

Another frequent mistake is considering that there are moments
where it is important to work the network. For instance, in a particular
month of the year, whereas there are other moments during which
we can ignore it.

Networking is a continuous activity, which should be the focus of our
attention on a daily basis, because opportunities don't keep a schedule. They simply appear in front of those prepared to see them.

Networking isn't for everyone

Across my relations, there is always someone who comes up and
says: «In my area of business, networking is not necessary, since I
don't sell anything».

There are several inherent misconceptions about this statement:

• There is no longer such a thing as a lifetime job. Meaning that in
  five or ten years' time it is quite possible that we will be doing
  something that we didn't even imagine as possible.

• Even in the work we perform today, we do not hold a total knowledge, since throughout the world, there is always someone with
  more knowledge or able to do it better. Therefore, it may prove
  quite useful not to despise this knowledge.

- Networking is not exclusive for salespeople, although it usually is easier to explain the importance of networking to commercial teams, since their monthly income is directly linked to the way they work their contact network.

Notwithstanding, they are not the only ones reaping the benefits.

I have met several professionals that claim to be aware of networking, going as far as saying that they are quite good at this activity. Nevertheless, when I watch them in action, I can verify that they look like kids collecting stickers, because they hand out and receive cards as if they were dealing with a football sticker collection.

Your goal during a networking event should not be going out the door holding X cards and with Y cards distributed. Just as in other areas of life, what is really important is the quality of contacts and not the quantity.

This behavior of handing out and receiving cards at great speed has two counterproductive effects:
- self-depreciation of the person who does it;
- depreciation of the interlocutor.

It is not a good idea to start a relationship by depreciating ourselves and depreciating the person in front of us.

Networking is about giving cards quickly

There is a general belief that we only need to be present at a given networking event to have immediate access to opportunities. It may happen, but only by a chance of luck.

According to my own personal experience, I've learnt that luck is made, only as a result of actions, but no points are obtained only by our mere presence. Therefore, it is important to take the initiative, without being afraid or embarrassed.

Bearing this in mind, when we are attending a cocktail party, a conference or any sort of networking event and we interact with someone, even if for a short period of time, we have to be present, i.e. we must focus our entire attention on that person and not think about where the shrimp cocktail we like so much is being served!!

The important thing is to be present

Networking? For what?

Background

Networking is something we perform on a daily basis and quite natu-rally. However, without clear objectives networking becomes an activ-ity without major results. For that reason, it is necessary to establish clear objectives, so we are able to define the correct actions.

What goals should
I expect from
networking?

Basically, there are four great objectives of networking:
• to search for business opportunities;
• to search for friendship or even romantic relationships;
• to search for a job;
• to access new knowledge.

Making business

Creation of a business opportunity has always been the most popu-lar application of networking. The idea is to publicize that I offer a given product or service and, through the network, that same mes-sage will reach potential clients/users.

A successful businessperson likes to discuss and participate in cer-tain activities that apparently are in no way related to business; golf-ing, frequently attending certain dinners, keeping a season ticket for home games of his/her favorite team, etc.

This happens because golf courses, stadiums, restaurants and other venues have become great places for business.

Nevertheless, making business depends mainly on the focus we maintained in our goals. For that reason, don't worry, because you don't have to excel in golf; leave those glories to those more inter-ested in this game.

The entire society soon realized that the celebration of the happiness of others – weddings, baptisms and other ceremonies – creates an environment prone to the creation of new relationships.

In these situations, the important thing is to remain fully aware of the objectives that first lead us to attend such celebrations and to act accordingly.

Do you dance?

In a period of crisis, many turn to networking as if it was a religion, able to provide comfort during hard times.

Networking might be extremely useful to find job opportunities, but we shouldn't seem desperate in our attempt to find a job. The world only likes desperate people in television game shows, not in real life.

If your objective is to find a new job, it will be quite important to follow these pieces of advice:

A new job

- Don't badmouth your current or previous employer. As one often says: «He who chatters with you, will chatter about you.»

- Choose the targets of your contacts well: don't shoot at random.

- Contact by voice the contacts that you are more at ease with; don't send out emails with the title «I need a job».

- Ask for advice, don't ask for jobs. Everybody loves to give advice but may feel rather embarrassed when unable to help right away. Therefore, save your interlocutor the embarrassment; if he/she is able to help on an immediate basis, he/she will certainly do so.

- Study, read books and articles, take part in training sessions, i.e., do whatever you can to keep up-to-date and open to new opportunities.

- Attend networking events or create your own, socialize, talk to people; do not barricade yourself inside your comfort zone.

- Broadly speaking, act professionally in all your interactions; for instance, if you make a commitment to send your curriculum vitae today, really send it.

Using other people's
brains

We are surrounded by information. Never as today has it been possible to find so much information regarding so many matters and there seems to be more and more each day. Information is no longer a scarce resource. Now it is something that floods over us, and we are having increasing difficulties filtering it.

How does one deal with this daily tsunami of information? One thing is for sure: Solutions from past centuries no longer work. We need to act accordingly in order to utilize information correctly.

We must look at social networks and work them as the Internet works computer networks.

We are all aware that there is a single computer that contains the entire content of the Web; that content is scattered along a myriad of computer networks that are connected amongst themselves.

Currently, human beings are more connected. However there is no one capable of absorbing the entire knowledge related to a given theme; therefore, it is increasingly more important to be connected with people who complement our knowledge, instead of having the fantasy of accumulating the all knowledge ourselves.

Presently, there are means and platforms that allow us to create our own search engine.

Think about it: When you insert a given concept into a search engine like Google, it will find millions of references. Many of these are useless for your particular case, because the categorization was made by computer applications. Nevertheless, a minute-long conversation with the right person might help you find the needle in the haystack almost instantly.

In order to achieve this, whenever needed, one needs to work the network skillfully. This is made quite easy with professional social networks within the so-called Web 2.0.

Personal management of knowledge will undoubtedly become the greatest expanding area of networking; we only need to regard the overwhelming rhythm of growth in available information.

Offer a refresher! FREE a

References Sell. They Sell a Lot!!!

There is no emotional transfer when we let computers buy from each other. All purchases made between humans are an emotional transfer; in his book 'Descartes' Error', Professor António Damásio clearly proves that there aren't strictly rational decisions.

For that reason, the best salespeople of our products and services are our clients, with whom we must keep continuous and fruitful relations for all concerned.

Let us see some simple and efficient ways of working our references.

Background

Regardless of the number of clients, colleagues, suppliers and other people eventually connected with us, we must gather information on every interaction, so that we may use it in future communications..

And what information should be gathered? All that could be considered useful. Let me provide some examples:

• Contact data: Address, phone, mobile phone, email, website.

• Personal data: Birthday, name of spouse and children, relevant family data, hobbies, likes, team preferences, associations' membership.

• Commercial data: Purchases performed, interest demonstrated in given products.

• Professional data: Current and previous positions.

Such a database should be, to a certain degree, decentralized; otherwise it would be an impossible task for SME and individuals. Thus, how do we decentralize?

Make your contact work for you. We may have:

• Contact data in a fairly common software, such as Outlook.

• Personal data through a profile within sites such as Hi5, MySpace, Facebook, etc.

• Commercial data in appropriate commercial management software programs.

Having a top-of-the-line database

• Professional data through a profile within sites such as Linkedin, Plaxo, Xing, etc.

The greatest advantage behind this decentralization is that the data is updated by the contact himself, through social networks. In later chapters, we will deal with the possibilities of social networks that are a revolution in the way we establish relationships.

Working on the database

An out-of-date database is a nullity; it is valued by its degree of up-to-dateness and so dedicate some time updating your database, eventually getting involved in others where your clients and potential clients might be.

This is, in fact, a never-ending task, but very rewarding when done properly.

Keeping in touch with the references

Don't allow your better references to become simple contacts, more or less anonymous within an immense database.

Maintain contact with your references – write an email, phone, get-together with them.

Don't forget the effort you've made to have these people as your references.

With a small parcel of that initial effort, you may improve their quality and achieve good outcomes.

Pamper

Surprise your contacts by personally giving them a souvenir, tickets for a concert with their favorite singer, a phone call on their birthday, organize get-togethers... In a nutshell, use your imagination, because a little treat is not a question of having or not having a budget.

Your goal should be turning a mere contact into a long-lasting relationship; to achieve that, use the most powerful weapon – asking your contacts for advice on:

- How you can improve your products or services;
- How should you face current market conditions;
- How to reach specific market niches;
- Etc.

At the end of this process, you will witness a greater involvement, but do keep in mind to make sure to follow-up, demonstrate that you took into consideration the advice given when the time comes to make decisions. The same goes for sharing your successes with your references.

Transforming
a contact into
a relationship

NETWORKING
OPPORTUNITIES

Where Do You Belong Within the Network?

Before assembling any strategy whatsoever and even before establishing a purpose, we need to understand what position we occupy within the networks we integrate and also to determine the position of those connected to us.

It is quite interesting to realize which people will potentially have the greatest impact in our lives.

Background

Generally speaking, we often consider that the people with a greater impact on our lives are those who belong to our natural network, that is composed of three types of people:
• friends;
• family members;
• colleagues.

In case of need, the usual situation is that we resort to our natural network, for instance, when we need a job.

Nevertheless, our natural network is usually widely limited, since our friends are familiar with each other, just as our family members and colleagues. Therefore a message made available in our natural network will tend to flow within a closed circuit.

Natural network

Broadly speaking, we can say that social networks are made of interconnected nodes. These nodes might fit two types:
• Contacts – nodes with only a few connections.
• Hubs – nodes with plenty of connections.

Hubs are people able to work the network in an extraordinary manner. They are the types that everybody knows in high school, in a village, in a city, in a country, in a continent or in the world.

They are the people who have power and influence that is above average. Their opinions or recommendations to people, companies, products or services have huge leverage.

Some of these hubs have become increasingly more powerful, largely thanks to the media (a prime example in the USA is Oprah

Hubs

Winfrey who has a legion of followers buying everything she endorses but she isn't considered the world's most powerful woman by chance).

Figure 2.1 Oprah Winfrey's page on Wikipedia (www.wikipedia.org)

The secret of «weak ties»

Right now you're probably thinking «What I really need is to get out of my natural network and become connected with a hub!» and, indeed, you're thinking wisely. But how do you do that?

Let me introduce to you a very valuable concept, the concept of «weak tie». A «weak tie» is a contact outside our natural network, someone we meet at any given social event, someone we passed by only for brief minutes, with whom we exchanged cards, i.e., someone with whom we do not have a strong relationship.

So what is the real importance of «weak ties»? They allow us to step outside of our natural network and to establish a contact with their networks, which, by definition, are made of people we don't know.

Several studies of social networks proved that the biggest business or entrepreneurship opportunities come forward mainly through «weak ties» and not through natural networks.

In other words, despite the weakness of ties, these should be treated as pure gold, because these are the people we may pass by every single day; as a result, we should be very careful with the first impression we create.

But be aware: The outcomes of those «weak ties» are not immediate, they might suffer a delay, i.e., a month or a year after that random encounter you might receive a phone call that will change your life.

To be able to become connected with weak ties, you need to step outside of you comfort zone, which means, for instance, that when you attend a party, a conference or any other event, you will have to address people you wouldn't normally address.

Step outside your comfort zone

It is quite easy to fall into the trap of talking to someone we already know, because they belong to our comfort zone. But we need to keep in mind that we are losing opportunities to connect with contact networks that go beyond our natural network.

A simple piece of advice: During the next event, if you feel shy or embarrassed to talk to someone, make your move at that precise moment; don't think it over, – talk! With enough practice, you'll see that it becomes increasingly easier.

How Can I Create Networking Opportunities?

Some people in this world are already born with an extraordinary contact network, because their family has already created such a network. For that reason, we're familiar with plenty of stories of families that lost everything due to wars and sudden political changes. But a couple of years later, they recovered their previous financial status.

Background

The vast majority of people aren't born with such a valuable contact network and, as a result, we have to look around and understand how to create networking opportunities, with the final objective of creating and maintaining contact networks.

One needs to realize that networking opportunities are not just ways of meeting people. They are also moments during which we might be under the observation of very important people for our careers and therefore it is important to keep an honest and coherent attitude at all times.

Conferences

Many conferences are worth our while for their coffee breaks or lunches rather than for the contents presented. Being fully aware of this fact, the promoters of such events are now including moments, and even special areas, specifically dedicated to networking, where, through the information included during the enrolment process, participants are grouped according to common interests.

Here is what you can do in order to improve your networking skills during events:

- ARRIVE BEFORE THE STARTING TIME – this will allow you to be truly familiar with the venue and to perceive exactly how everything will be performed, apart from allowing you also to interact with some participants and even the speakers, if they are the punctual type.

- TALK TO THE PROMOTERS – not only will this provide you with information about the event, it will also allow you to help other participants and even speakers, thus being regarded as a nice and well informed person.

- DEFINE YOUR TARGETS – some days earlier, define and study the people you want to talk to – speakers, participants and exhibitors.

- KEEP YOUR BUSINESS CARDS AT HAND – carry a fair amount of business cards and be prepared to receive as many.

- STUDY THE EXHIBITORS PLAN AND EXHIBITION SCHEDULES – thus, you will be able to speak to exhibitors outside the rush hours. You are not there to get freebies; you're there for business and so you should reserve some quality time to visit stands that appeal you the most.

- MINGLE – your time is your most scarce resource, use it well. Being careful with the time spent in each interaction and try to assess the interest of each one during the first minutes. Don't waste time interacting with your colleagues.

- KEEP YOUR BADGE VISIBLE – we all love being called by our own name and we should bear that in mind while addressing others.

- QUESTION – put forward relevant questions to the speakers during and after interventions, because not only this is a way to take a greater advantage of the conference, it is also a way to be remembered by other participants and speakers.

- BREAKS ARE NOT USED FOR WORK – forget the office. These days, during a break, it is very curious to observe the dynamics of participants. It looks something like a race to mobile phones or computers, when nothing could be more urgent than to achieve the goals of your presence in the conference. By the way, how many times do you pick up your phone simply not to talk to strangers?

- TAKE NOTES – when interacting with someone, write the most interesting facts on that person's business card. Also make notes on the speakers' notes, but don't write every detail.

And, why not, organize your own conferences...

....

Training

Whether it is a few hours course or a degree, this is a fabulous networking opportunity during which we can establish contact with people who share similar aspirations, both with fellow participants but also with trainers and teachers. And the longer it lasts, the stronger will the ties be.

Moreover, some actions have residential characteristics, thus formenting networking among students and teachers.

There isn't a generalized conscience among students on how many opportunities are lost throughout life as a consequence of behaviors that label them among peers and teachers.

For instance: how many of us would provide a good reference of that high school friend who was a compulsive liar although twenty years have passed? This behavior will forever affect our vision of this colleague.

As a teacher and a trainer, I have had thousands of students and trainees; nevertheless, I can only recall the extremes, the underachievers and the overachievers, without any correlation to given grades. I remember the attitudes that struck me the most: Honesty, straightforwardness, argumentation skills, falsehood, dishonesty, etc...

When attending a course, we must also keep a professional attitude, since we will be judged for our posture during many years and this may open or close doors.

Fortunately, awareness is increasing about the effects of networking in training, f.i. by establishing groups of professionals truly interested in personal and professional development. It is not a random fact that the training courses generate added value, – professionals usually and continuously repeat that one of the most attractive highlights of training courses is the generated networking, surely responsible for years and years of opportunities.

An example of this reality is the former Harvard and IESE's MBA students that get together on a regular basis. You can be sure that dinner is not the only thing on the menu.

Advice for those attending training courses:

- Choose the contents, the format and the teachers, carefully, as to achieve your life goals.
- You're investing, so your main effort should be how to obtain revenue, making it more demanding.
- Be professional, you're fulfilling a goal, and its fulfillment won't be necessarily judged by grades.
- Use training as a lab to improve skills such as team work, active listening, presentation techniques, etc.
- Seize every moment to learn, do not study for the sake of studying.
- Research, create new concepts, all according to your objectives.
- Be available to help your peers and teachers.
- Organize extracurricular activities to strengthen the ties created in the classroom.
- Try to maintain a relationship with peers and teachers even after the course has finished. If you managed to accomplish the previous points, these contacts will be worth gold.

Speed networking

Speed networking events copy the logic of other older events like speed dating, where people try to meet a potential love partner.

Speed networking events come from the awareness that other events such as cocktail parties, conferences and like such have a minute networking component, even being quite limited as far as number of interactions goes.

During a speed networking event, the number of participants is obtained according to the available time, because they are invited to sit in front of each other, paired up, and to provide a brief explanation of their occupation. After 5 minutes have passed, very loud music begins with the objective of stopping all conversations and to force people to change pairs. This way, it is possible to ensure interaction with 12 people within an hour period.

Preparation is essential for speed networking events, because we only have an average of two and a half minutes to clearly explain what we do and what we intend. Business cards are a must.

We must try to have a two and a half minute speech ready, so that we don't have any trouble repeating it over twelve times. We must also know how to listen to our interlocutor, because our speech may need to be adapted to the nature of his speech.

Last but not the least is the follow-up, which will consolidate the contacts established during the event. This is the stage that makes all the difference. The follow-up may be performed by email, phone or even in person.

Being a part of associations creates excellent networking opportunities. Whether these are residents', parents' associations, former students, classroom, former military, religious or political associations, all allows us to acquaint and become acquainted.

We must be careful when choosing associations and therefore it is necessary:

to somehow relate to the official values and ideals. It is counterproductive to be a part of an association with which we cannot relate.

not just to pay the fees. Being a member of an association without regularly taking part in its activities is an expensive nullity.

to somehow contribute to the life of the association. Make a commitment to try and help improve the association through concrete ideas.

to develop activities within the association. The creation of new initiatives will surely open doors to new opportunities.

Becoming a part
of associations

Figure 2.2. Former ISEG Students Association (http://alumni.iseg.utl.pt)

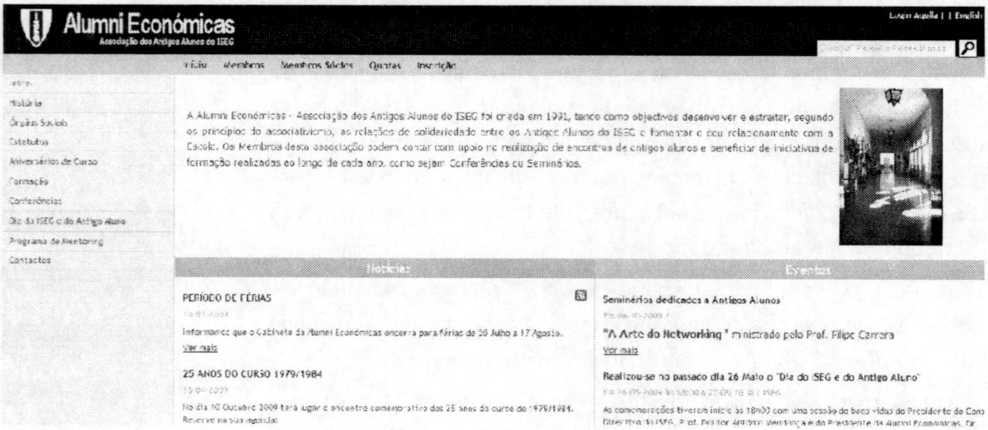

Social events

Lunches, dinners, cocktail parties, weddings, baptisms and other social events always had a mission: to act as excuses so that people could get together and do business.

Does this mean that we have to be ready for networking at all times? Yes! Every moment may contain great opportunities and so preparation is essential (for instance, don't leave the house without your business cards).

We must also divide our attention by the greatest possible number of people, but quality attention. Even if we only spend thirty seconds with a person, it is important to focus entirely on him but not on the surrounding environment.

A small trick: During professional cocktail parties, always grab a bite to eat before attending because you don't want to be betrayed by your stomach, having to divide your attention between the need to eat and the need to establish contacts.

Mind the drinks: Nothing will destroy a person's reputation any faster than being clearly under the influence of alcohol.

Volunteer work often is associated with the solving of social problems, such as poverty or drug addiction. Nevertheless, becoming a
volunteer could be much more: It might become a way to create a
space to showcase our talents.

Volunteer work

For instance, I've been attending, since 2002, ASTD's – American
Society for Training and Development (www.astd.org) – renowned
annual international conference and I always meet some people, all
well above their thirties and holding plaques saying «Ask me!»; these
are the people providing information on room location, schedules
and other useful information.

During the first year, I didn't pay much attention to the fact, but during
the second year I realized that, although the conference was in a different city and state, the volunteers were the same; for this reason, I
decided to look further into the reasons behind such dedication.

While talking to the volunteer workers, I quickly understood their motivations:

• The volunteers had the possibility to attend part of the conference
  without paying any fees, i.e., they paid with their work for the conference.

• The volunteers worked as a group of friends who rendezvoused
  once a year, so this was an extraordinary moment of camaraderie
  and clearly of networking among professionals in the human
  resources and training industry that, if this hadn't happened,
  would not had even meet.

Another association I'm a part of is JCI – Junior Chamber International (www.jci.cc), which is based on the volunteer work of its members to perform all initiatives, thus achieving the goal behind its creation: To provide young people, aged 18 to 40, the opportunity to
develop their leadership skills.

Offer your competences and free time to causes in which you believe. You will see that this is a fantastic opportunity to step outside
your natural network, to make acquaintances and become acquainted.

Although we're dealing with volunteer work, don't forget to act professionally; remember that we are always being watched.

Figure 2.3. JCI's website – Junior Chamber International (www.jci.cc)

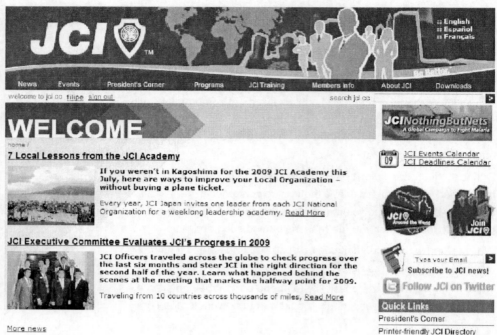

Become a speaker   Always be available as a speaker to share your experience with oth-
                        ers in public events.

                        Being a speaker is like driving. The more you practice, the easier it
                        gets. Nevertheless, it is better to be familiar with some techniques
                        and, hence, I leave you some practical advice:

                        • Observe other successful speakers, but do not mimic them, try to
                          create your own style.

                        • Take a course on presentation techniques. You'll see that you'll
                          learn a lot about yourself.

                        • Do your homework before giving a presentation. Study the sub-
                          jects, the audience and its objectives.

                        • Start a dialogue with the organization – clearly define the equip-
                          ment available for the presentation, the room layout, schedules,
                          the way the event will be publicized and the number of expected
                          participants.

- Avoid school-type classes. Take advantage of the knowledge within the audience and interact.

- Attend the presentations of previous speakers, in order to assess the audience's reactions.

- In your mind, visualize your communication; include the smiles of people satisfied with what you shared.

- Being a speaker is not an award, it is a responsibility and your responsibility is to bring something useful to your audience and not to solely demonstrate your wisdom.

- Maintain a positive and confident attitude and, most of all, keep in mind that 80% of communication is non-verbal communication.

- Use the audiovisuals aids at your disposal proficiently, avoid death by PowerPoint.

- Linger a little longer after your communication; use breaks to talk to participants, to receive and deliver business cards and to obtain comments or suggestions about what you just said since there's always room for improvement.

- Finally, be as natural as possible, using the resources that best fit your personality.

Being a speaker allows you to concentrate on contacts and to assume an expert position within the integrated network, as well as to become exposed to other networks.

Writing articles for the media has a double advantage:

Writing articles

- The most obvious one is to increase our level of market exposure, allowing us to become recognized as experts.

- It also forces us to be continuously up-to-date, to study our questions, to have new ideas.

The media are thirsty for contents and so there are plenty of opportunities to write in newspapers and magazines. Begin with local social media, to get used to deadlines and to the discipline behind this type of writing.

Articles may even give origin to a book, which is a great medium to work the contact network.

| Having a mentor and becoming a mentor | Having a mentor is a privilege; it allows us to have the dispassionate advice of someone who has the necessary distance to state true facts that we might even dislike hearing but will be useful, if we are humble enough to accept them. |

Simultaneously, a mentor has his own contact network, with which we will certainly connect.

On the other hand, becoming a mentor of other professionals is an opportunity to mark our professional life in a good sense and, quite logically, to become associated with their outcomes, also allowing you to contact with the networks of these professionals.

| Social media | Web social networks or social media offer an array of tools to efficiently deal with our contacts and increase our network. |

In Chapter 6, I will approach in greater detail the main potentials of these new means, but for now, it is important to bear in mind that social media tools must be associated with the above mentioned networking opportunities.

For example, while organizing an event of any sort, I must associate my contact network through a page that will allow me to notify them, as well as gather, for instance, registrations.

International Networking

| Background | Over the last few years, I have provided training in about 40 countries, scattered around 4 continents, and therefore dealt with many different cultures. That is the experience I wish to share with you. |

All the opportunities I had to work outside of Portugal were the result of an intense networking effort on my part and of the deep understanding of the realities of my interlocutors.

I will now leave you with some practical advice, which has proven to be quite useful.

As human beings the word we like most is our name. As citizens of a country we enjoy seeing our country recognized by foreigners.

I can't fight the urge of telling a small personal story. When I first started my career as a financial analyst, I had the chance to attend an English course. During one of the classes the teacher decided to give a general knowledge competition in English.

For me, this was very amusing, because I mastered the entire competition. At a given moment, the question was «What is the world's largest waterfall?» The more obvious answers came forward and I, certain of my answer, saved myself for last and firmly stated: «Salto del Angel, in Venezuela!»

At this moment, the teacher, already somewhat annoyed by my consecutive right answers, asked what the height of that waterfall was and I answered «979 meters!»

Her comment was: «You're full of useless knowledge!» to whichI replied «Someday, it will be useful!» And, my dear reader, I was right.

Being familiar with general knowledge issues about a country we work with or visit opens many doors, makes us understand the reason behind the things we witness and, most importantly, it demonstrates a deep respect for other individuals.

At the time of the competition I just described, my tools only included books that I read passionately and the media. But the coming of the web has made things a lot easier. Websites like Wikipedia or Google Maps, among others, are essential to rapidly become familiar with history and geography issues of countries and territories.

Know your history and geography

Figure 2.4. Gathering information on countries (www.wikipedia.org)

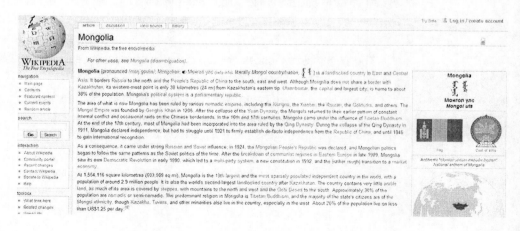

Know some words
of the language

In 1992, I was a senior at my Economics studies at ISEG and president of the Senior Students Commission, whose main objective was to plan a students' trip.

Since I was never a big fan of travelling thousands of miles just to go to the beach, I yearned for a journey that would have a personal meaning and, therefore, when a colleague suggested Cuba, a country that at that time was taking its first steps in tourism, I gladly accepted the idea.

Given that in the early 1990s there were no such thing as organized trips to Cuba; I decided to go to the Cuban Embassy in Lisbon, filled with good will and high proficiency of Spanish. At the time, only a few people were able to go further than «Spanguese» (a hybrid between Portuguese and Spanish).

From the very first moment on, I had a deep empathy by the embassy's staff, which resulted in a visit to the home of the Cuban ambassador, only for the pleasure of discussing foreign politics.

With this experience, I learned that language is the key to the soul and ever since I've incessantly tried to learn some words of all languages spoken in the countries I visit.

Recently, I had the opportunity to be a main coach for a Mongolian leadership academy and I was called, along with my translator, onto the stage to address the Mongolian audience. I focused my speech around the Mongolian word for «thank you», that I deliberately repeated over a dozen times in my speech with the best possible pronunciation. This created an extraordinary emotional bond with the audience.

Thanks to situations like this, I often leave countries with relations that go beyond mere contacts, thus ensuring my return for further jobs.

The Web makes the task of learning some words quite easy I'll give you two practical examples:

iTunes – by using this program, you can download podcasts, featuring basic language courses, into your computer, iPod or iPhone. If you ever come across me in an airport and I have earphones, I'm probably learning a new language.

Language websites – Google features an interesting translating tool, but I prefer websites like Travlang which not only teaches us how to write basic words, it features recordings with pronunciation, which is a great way of surprising our hosts.

Figure 2.5. At Travlang, it is possible to learn the pronunciation of words in more than 70 languages (www.travlang.com)

1. SELECT A LANGUAGE YOU SPEAK: English

2. SELECT THE LANGUAGE YOU WANT TO LEARN:
(Organized alphabetically)

How many misunderstandings and even wars were caused as a consequence of the lack of knowledge of customs and traditions?

In 2007, I was attending a Conference in Cairo. I had already delivered my speech and I was sitting in the front row watching the intervention of a friend and colleague, who was sitting normally with his

Traditions

legs crossed in such a fashion that the soles of his shoes were showing to an audience of 250 Arabs.

Knowing how insulting this gesture is in the Arab world, I did everything within my reach to pass the message to my colleague, and he
finally put his foot down, before any major problem arose

The more distant the countries are, the bigger the probability of gestures and attitudes being considered totally friendly in some places,
and considered insulting in other places and vice-versa.

Using web tools and some books, it is a good idea to know the traditions of the countries we visit and of the people who visit us.

Nevertheless, it is necessary to bear in mind that certain traditions
grow flexible as people become more acquainted with one another.

In 2005, I visited Japan in order to attend a course and I bought a
travelling guide that I read avidly before my arrival at Osaka. That
guide, similar to everything else I had read so far, stated over and
over again that physical contact must be avoided with Japanese people, because it is something quite embarrassing to them.

After arriving, I kept my distances. I took bows from different angles,
received and offered business cards with both hands, ate using chop
sticks, etc. I did everything according to the text book, but the text
book failed to mention that, after a day's work, what the Japanese
most enjoy would be to go to a bar and drink incredible amounts of
alcohol. And you can be sure that after a night out like this the physical contact rule only made sense in the text book.

Therefore and as a start-up, it is important to strictly follow the traditions, regarding them as a manifestation of respect. You may, nevertheless, become more flexible if your hosts demonstrate such open-
ness.

We live in a small global village

I've always heard that we live in a small world and I´ve felt this in several different ways, but in one particular situation, it overcame my
own limits.

During my participation at a Japanese Kobe academy, the first three
days were spent at the house of a Japanese couple, thus giving me
the chance to be minimally integrated within the Japanese way of life.

As I said, I stayed with a nice Japanese couple who picked me up at
the hotel, where the training sessions over the next days would be

held, and due to great communication difficulties, the ride home was made almost in silence.

When entering the apartment, I was surprised by a properly framed puzzle depicting Porto's D. Luís Bridge; in the hall, I also found some Portuguese tiles and several typically Portuguese objects could be found elsewhere in the apartment. In awe, I asked them if they had ever gone to Portugal and they answered that yes, they had been there three times now, since their daughter had lived in Portugal for ten years.

They quickly fetched their daughter's card, which featured her address. After picking the card up, I tried to follow Japanese protocol, holding the card with both hands and taking a small vow, but what came next broke all protocols.

While I was reading their daughter's card, I couldn't hold myself and burst out into laughter, apologizing in between the laughs. When I was finally able to control my laughter, I explained the reason for my behavior. Their daughter now lived at number 29 inthe same street where I grew up and lived until I got married, and my father still lives at number 4, from where we can clearly see their daughter's home.

Right now, we are capable of shrinking the world by using social networks and cheaper transportations.

Something I persistently do with my contacts, whether personally by phone or in writing, is to check their profile and add them to my contacts.

This allows for a follow-up process and a reinforcement of the ties that, a couple of years ago, were unthinkable, – by creating our own world, in which people who live thousands of miles away can be closer than those living only a couple of meters from us.

As a gastronome, whenever I'm abroad, I never order my own food. I've learned that, consciously or unconsciously, we tend to order the courses we already know or those we're already accustomed to, thus missing the opportunity of interesting discoveries.

Golden rule

Consequently, I have a golden rule that I apply on my travels and that can be summarized as follows: «I follow the natives».

Practically speaking, I leave every decision in the hands of my hosts: where I go, what I eat, what I see, demonstrating some particular interest here and there.

Once again, this type of attitude demonstrates respect and trust in the other person, which will be the basis for transforming a simple contact into a relationship.

3

YOUR PRESENTATION

Preparation

Sun Tzu used to say: «Every battle is won before it is even fought» and this is an absolute truth when we're dealing with networking.

Some people attend networking events and claim that they never achieve great results. When I investigate a little further, I realise that the preparation effort was close to nothing.

Without preparation, the chances of success are identical to a lottery, so it is important to do our homework properly.

Background

Attending a networking event is not sufficient to obtain results; therefore, previous analysis is needed, one that allows us to decide, in the first place, if our presence is really worth it. If indeed it is worth it, what will we do?

When analyzing an event, one must consider the following aspects:

- TYPE OF EVENT – dinner, conference, speed networking, etc.
- AVAILABLE INFORMATION – Leaflet, venue, social network page, etc.
- PARTICIPANTS – profiles of the people attending the event (promoters, participants and speakers).
- LOCATION – access, centrality or remoteness.
- CHARACTERIZATION OF THE VENUE – Hotel, auditorium, restaurant, exclusive or public space, etc.
- REGISTRY – open to the public; for registered participants; cost--free or not; registry method, etc.
- ACCESS TO PARTICIPANTS AND SPEAKERS DATA – Access prior to, during or after the event; no access to data.

After establishing these elements, we are able to engage in a finer analysis.

Analysis of events

Analysis of participants

It is possible that we might never have access to precise information on the participants of a given event, but we must try to gather as much information as possible, using, among other things, the following means:

- A list of previous participants.
- Information gathered on our contact network, regarding their information on the event.
- Research on search engines and social networks.

The objective is to know clearly, before arriving at the event, who will be attending and whether or not the participants' objectives are in tune with ours.

Setting goals

Establishing goals before entering a given networking event is the key to success. It is also the way to perform an objective assessment of the event from our point of view.

What objective must we have in a networking event? I mention the following as examples:

- To meet given people.
- To explain our new project to professionals from a given industry.
- To obtain contacts.
- To chat with specific targets, which are considered as priorities.
- To raise awareness of a new product or service.

By being fully aware of our objectives, it necessary to assess if the event will allow us, to begin with, to achieve our objectives. Otherwise, it is probably better to choose a different event.

Facing an audience

In some events, we might be invited to speak to audiences with variable dimensions and, often, this comes as a surprise. Therefore, it is necessary to have our «spontaneous communication» properly studied and prepared.

To achieve such, it is important to be prepared with some elements:

- OUR PRESENTATION – who we are, what we do, why we are attending the event.

- WHAT WE WANT TO SELL – our company, products, services, ourselves.

- MATERIAL – our presentation may include materials which need to be printed or recorded beforehand.

The preparation of the abovementioned elements will make us feel safe in front of any audience (whether it is a group at a dining table or in an auditorium).

We must take proper caution in finding out what the most suitable dress code is for each event, because dressing inappropriately will create empathy problems with the other participants, as well as an undermining of self-confidence.

Dress Code

The following table puts forward a simplified scale of dress codes:

Dress Code	Description
Casual	Casual pants and polo shirt or shirt.
Business casual	Informal wear with a professional touch as, for instance, a coat.
Business	The famous suit and tie and the equivalent in women's wear.
Formal	Smoking, tuxedo, and evening gown for the ladies.

Can we prepare self-confidence? Yes, we indeed can by:

Self-confidence

- Analyzing the event.
- Analyzing the participants.
- Clearly defining our goals.
- Preparing our presentation ahead of time.
- Dressing accordingly.

If even so you feel nervous, try a simple exercise before entering the event venue:

- straighten your back;
- discreetly rotate the upper part of your arms to the back, with emphasis on your collar bone and in order to fill your chest;
- smile;
- now you're ready to enter.

In my understanding, there is a word that perfectly symbolizes what happens when we establish contacts during a networking event: The word is flirting. We are transmitting our image, the image of our corporation, of our products, with the final purpose of captivating potential clients.

Networking Accessories

Background

Some years ago, whenever networking accessories were mentioned, one was able to summarize them in business cards and pen. Today, one must rethink those accessories and search for others.

At this point, it is important to be prepared beforehand, i.e., to know what needs to be taken to a networking event, but also to know how to use what is taken, thus avoiding situations where we find ourselves carrying certain objects simply because other people also carry them.

The indispensable business card

The business card first appeared in China during the 15th century, being introduced in Europe two centuries later. What's interesting to know is that this essential networking accessory did not evolve much throughout time.

The structure and information on your business card must be considered in great detail, bearing in mind the final recipients. Traditionally, business cards include the following elements:
- name;
- position held within the organization;

- name of organization, logo, slogan, mission;
- address;
- telephone, fax, mobile/cell phone;
- web address;
- email address;
- license, work permit, number of professional identification card.

Business cards need new elements, since they are essential to establish contacts between professionals:

New elements on business cards

- INSTANT MESSAGING ADDRESS – Do you have an MSN, Skype or similar account? Don't hide it. The important thing is to be reachable when your contact needs you the most and by the most convenient means.

- SAY WHAT YOUR REAL FUNCTION IS – don't just and exclusively state a position on the organization chart.

- GPS COORDINATES – with the widespread use of GPS devices, it may be quite helpful to indicate the coordinates: Clients and suppliers are able to get to our facilities quickly, particularly when they're on a recent industrial or housing complex.

- PICTURE – picture of the person holding the card and it is advisable that the picture conveys the values we want to transmit. A photo with a good definition so that the person can be easily identified. Have your photo in black and white, thus avoiding weird contrasts between what you are wearing on the picture and the organization's colors.

Placing your photo on your business card is quite controversial and there is some heavy resistance to this inclusion; therefore, a vast majority of companies do not include this feature.

My photo on my business card?

According to my understanding, this is a mistake and to prove my point, I will provide you with two examples of common behavior:

- When writing a note, a letter or an email message, we naturally visualize the recipient in our mind and inclusively his/her reaction.

- When we attend a networking event, having received dozens of business cards, we observe them after the event, and we also try to connect the names to the faces of the people we met.

This means that, by not including our photograph, we are making the life of our potential clients, suppliers or partners more difficult. Is that really a smart move?

An argument against the placement of a picture, which I've heard repeatedly during my networking seminars, is that very few organizations or liberal professionals use this resource. My answer is always in the form of a question: «If we do something our competitor does not do, would we be winning a competitive advantage?»

We may prove it through the following picture, which is not an innovation. Except that, today, with the advance of digital imaging and image editing software it is extremely easy to insert a picture on a business card.

Figure 3.1 Example of business card from 1895 (SSA History Archives)

Business cards
archive

During my networking seminars, I always ask how participants manage to archive the hundreds of business cards they receive, and the answers go from stacking them on the desk to more sophisticated processes, which use appropriate alphabetical filing systems.

These systems are the most common, but unfortunately they are not the most efficient, because:
• They do not allow a quick access to information.
• They are not really portable.
• They facilitate the loss of contacts.

Consequently, I advise the use of business cards readers, which can be found almost everywhere. (own equipment or integrated within mobile phones as for instance some Sony Ericsson models or iPhone).

The main functions of business card readers include:
• Digital organization of contacts at a very good scanning rate.
• Key word search.
• Easy categorization of contacts.
• Synchronization of card data with electronic devices and software, such as Outlook.
• Back and front digitalization, resulting in a clear image of the card, including notes.
• Possibility of sending an image of the card to a third party using an email connection.

But we need to pay attention because with the increasing availability of business cards readers we need to make sure that our business cards are ready for digitalization and, therefore, it is convenient to avoid including the following elements:
• photographic backgrounds;
• small fonts;
• fonts not adapted to digital means.

As a rule of thumb, a card that can be easily read by a person will be easily digitalized, because if there is an element slightly difficult to perceive, it will become a problem for the reader.

Figure 3.2. Business card reader available at www.irislink.com

New business cards

Regardless of the sophistication of business card readers, I believe in the growing importance of virtual business cards, such as:

- Microsoft Outlook's Vcard – undoubtedly, one of the best ways to enter directly into our contacts' databases, where we can include all information regarded as relevant.

- Mobile phone agenda.

- Email signature, which should include all contact information.

- Aztec Code – a type of 2D barcode which provides more information that the traditional barcode. This code may be included in your business card or in other materials and, at the time, some mobile phones are already equipped to read such codes.

The greatest advantage in this type of virtual cards is the fact that they are able to reduce errors during the input of our data into our contacts' database, thus facilitating future contacts.

Figure 3.3. Aztec Barcode Editor, available at www.jaxo-systems.com

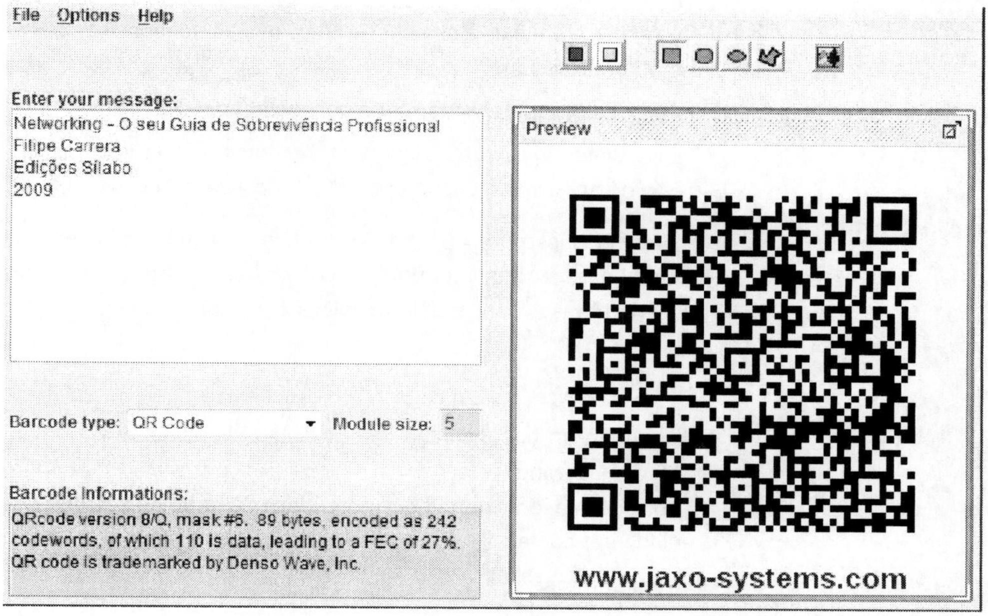

Mobile phones can be a magnificent networking accessory, if we are able to master it. Through infra-reds, Bluetooth or text messages we are able to pass our information to the contact's mobile phone.

Mobile phones aren´t just for calls

How often do we lose a good contact forever simply because we fail to write the correct number or we register the number, for instance, under the name «Ana» only to find out, a couple of weeks later, that we have another entrant with the same name.

A mobile phone has some other features that can also be useful:

• Camera – it allows us to take a picture that we can later associate to our agenda. But be careful; make sure to ask for your contact's permission.

• Aztec code reader.

• File synchronization – thus, one does not have to keep two or more agendas.

• Card reader.

Nevertheless, a mobile phone can sometimes be the reason for our failure in a networking event. Let me provide some examples:

- Taking the breaks to make phone calls implies not socializing with the other participants.
- It may inappropriately interrupt a conversation.
- It potentiates that, in the middle of the conversation, text messages are sent completely unrelated to the conversation.

We are the bosses of our mobile phones and not the other way around; therefore, it is important to know when to shut it down, because there was a world before mobile phones came into existence.

Schedules

Although I'm an unconditional fan of electronic schedules, particularly those allowing file synchronization, I recognize that some people, for one reason or another, prefer paper. The important thing is keeping your contacts efficiently organized.

Here's some advice regarding the use of electronic schedules:

- Input your contacts homogeneously, i.e., contact data must always be registered in the same fashion.
- Do not associate information or comments about contacts that you don't want others to see. Someday, you might share that contact and forget that that sort of comment was associated with the content.
- Backup frequently. Your schedule is an important part of your assets.
- Place your own contact information on the schedule, complete with the relevant data, as if it were one of your own contacts. This will allow you to share a virtual card to another person's schedule.

Badge

During a networking event, it is quite common to receive a badge containing your name and other information, with the objective of making conversation among participants a little easier.

Some advice following regarding the use of badges:

- Before accepting it, make sure the data shown is correct and, if some mistake is detected, request its substitution.
- Do not hide it: make it visible, always with the name facing forward.

- In certain more casual events, you can, and it is recommended, give it a personal touch, like coloring it, making a small drawing, a sticker or a pin. This will facilitate your identification and memorization by potential contacts.

- It is advisable to place the badge in areas of the body that do not cause people to get distracted.

Giveaways and gifts

We all love gifts and by living in a society in which it's harder and harder to know what to give, originality is more acknowledged than the money spent.

Therefore, small tokens and gifts can become much more useful to transform a contact into a relationship, particularly abroad.

Notwithstanding, we must first consider some previous questions regarding the recipients of the giveaways and gifts:

- Are you travelling by plane? Safety restrictions limit the transportation of liquids, sharp objects among others, in handbaggage.

- What is the people's gender? Some gifts are more appropriate for the ladies, whereas others are better for gentlemen.

- What is their religion? Certain religions prohibit the consumption of alcohol and of certain types of food.

- What is the connection? We must seek to establish a connection between the gift or giveaway and our products, services or company and express that connection while handing them out. This will enhance memorization. The ideal is that our logo or name is printed on the giveaway or present.

Other materials

There are other materials that we might take with us when attending networking events, things that contain the presentation of our products and services, such as:
- brochures;
- samples;
- CD or DVD;
- personalized pen drives;
- etc.

Verbal Communication

Background

Communication between humans is something extraordinary. This is because more emotion is transmitted than concepts, so the acting of selling is indeed an act of emotional transferring.

This does not mean, however, that verbal communication isn't important, but rather that verbal communication on its own is almost useless!

The first 60 seconds

Americans have an expression that mentions the «elevator pitch» that can be explained like this: Imagine that you walk into an elevator and that inside you find a person, who is completely alone. This person can be very important for your professional future. He/she pushes the button to the fifth floor and you're left with 60 seconds to make a good impression.

The majority of people leave those 60 seconds in the hands of fate, of spontaneous inspiration. Good networkers prepare in advance. The secret is to always be prepared to create a good impression, a good contact...

Preparation starts by self-analyzing your objectives and clearly defining what you're capable of doing. This, of course, does mean that you have to speak hastily to fit everything into 60 seconds.

Remember that, according to an old definition, you don't get a second chance at making a good first impression.

The words

Some specific advice on verbal communication, which represents about 7 percent of communication:

• You must adapt your speech to your listener.

• Always articulate words correctly; train your diction, if necessary.

• Be positive in what you say. In communication, you reap exactly what you sow.

• Be assertive, don't complicate things.

According to an UCLA (University of California, Los Angeles) study, about 38 percent of communication is delivered by the tone of voice and, therefore, it is important to pay attention to the way we make use of this tool. A wrong tone of voice may completely compromise the message we are trying to convey.

Train this exercise with a colleague, following these scripts:

- Script 1
    - — Colleague: «Will we have lunch at the usual place?»
    - — You: (with a smile) «Of course we will.»
- Script 2
    - — Colleague: «Will we have lunch at the usual place?»
    - — You: (with an angry tone) «Of course we will.»

Through this exercise, you can see that the text is exactly the same for both scripts, but if you ask your colleague for his/her opinion, you will see that he/she felt as if you called him/her stupid during script 2.

With this simple exercise, one makes it quite clear that the tone of voice may destroy or become a lifesaver when construing a message.

Tone of voice

One of the greatest difficulties we face is not knowing how to start a conversation. It's almost a painful event; therefore, the big question is always the same – what theme shall we choose?

Here are some suggestions:

- Analyze the person before engaging in a conversation; the behavior may indicate some preferences.
- Check for common interests; for instance, both of you are attending the same event and, likely, you probably share some interests.
- Be original: don't talk about the weather – ask for his/her opinion on the event and really listen!
- Ask for information regarding the event.
- When I realize that a potential contact is a foreigner, I try to greet him/her in his/her own language.

How to start a conversation

Know when
to be quiet

A misguided conception about conversations is that this is a competitive activity, where a prize is given to the person who talked the most.

Think about this: What's a person favorite subject? Himself! Who do we think the nicest people are? Those who listen to us!

That does not mean that you should stand still and be quiet; there is no such thing as communication without feedback, which may be transmitted verbally or nonverbally.

Active listening is not only important to make our listener feel good during the conversation, it is also extremely important to shape our verbal and nonverbal language. Active listening should take into account the interlocutor's nonverbal language that is able to reinforce, to contradict or to go further beyond what's being said.

We might say that active listening is listening to what is being said and what is not being said, and to process and to incorporate it in our verbal and nonverbal language.

The power of ☺

Humor is indeed a powerful tool in any sort of human relationship. We love to be with the people that make us smile, because, in practical terms, we love the endorphins this generates.

Notwithstanding, we need to exercise some caution. There are three taboo themes, as far as humor goes when establishing a first contact:
• Politics.
• Religion.
• Sex.

There is a fairly safe theme: Ourselves, especially when we're seeking a lifesaver in an embarrassing situation.

Some years ago, I was in Athens in a hotel room, working on my computer, when I decided to check the programme for the international meeting I was attending.

I verified that the first moment for the event was a welcome party, where a formal dress code was required. Five minutes before heading up to the hotel room where the party was being held, I put on my smoking and called the elevator.

After arriving at the room's entrance, I realized that everyone else was dressed quite casually and that I was the only one wearing a tuxedo; I quickly addressed the five people I had met the previous day in the hotel bar who explained that the bags of one of the special guests failed to arrive and that, subsequently, the organizations had decided to make the ambience more informal.

Feeling quite embarrassed, I decided to laugh the whole situation off, saying that I felt like a penguin and I started walking like one. This approach caused my acquaintances (currently dear friends) to react quite spontaneously, making the decision to become my security convoy; as a consequence, I entered the room greeting everyone in a presidential manner, surrounded by «bodyguards» who prevented all forms of direct contact by saying: «El presidente cannot be disturbed».

A potentially embarrassing episode turned out to be a landmark in my career, considering that the relationships created on that day were extraordinary.

Non-Verbal Communication

Nonverbal communication is the process of sending and receiving nonverbal signs. Nonverbal communication may be performed through gestures, postures, facial expressions and visual contact, representing 55 percent of communication between humans.

The way we dress, how we comb our hair and our general presentation is incorporated into nonverbal communication.

Background

A highly associated concept to a quality communication is empathy, meaning the capacity to share and understand our interlocutor's emotions and feelings, as if, deep inside, we were able to walk in the other person's shoes.

Creating empathy with our interlocutor is the objective behind any quality contact; therefore, verbal and nonverbal active listening plays an essential role.

Empathy

The body

Our body communicates in several ways:

- gestures;
- facial expressions;
- posture;
- breathing.

It is very important to perform the following exercise: Record your own presentation and analyze if your body language is aligned or not with your verbal communication.

The look

How often do you go into a shop and ask the salesperson if the product being sold is really good?

Let us try to rationally analyze this situation. Are you really waiting to see the salesperson saying something like:

- hypothesis 1: «This product really stinks, I'd rather have my children starving than selling you this product!»
- hypothesis 2: «This is a really good product!»

Clearly, we hope that the salesperson answers with hypothesis 2. Then, if we already know the answer, why do we bother asking the question? To use our private lie detector.

During this dialogue, our tendency will be to look into the salesperson's eyes and closely watch his/her nonverbal communication, with the objective of testing his/her honesty.

Due to shyness, some people avoid looking into another person's eyes during a conversation, which sends a subliminal message to the interlocutor: «I don't want people testing my sincerity.»

For this reason, it is not possible to communicate effectively without looking in the eyes; nevertheless, don't overdo it – the objective is to look loosely and not to stare at people.

Safety perimeter

Particularly during the first contacts, we must respect the individual safety perimeter. This distance may vary according to cultural factors and gender.

At this point, we witness our primitive reflexes. Try this: If during a normal conversation you're having while standing, you inadvertently get too close to your interlocutor; you will immediately watch a body defense reaction.

Although we might feel perfectly safe within a given environment, our primitive brain will always be alert; for that same reason, the productivity of someone who works with his back turned to the door is less than that of a worker facing the door.

The perimeter's diameter decreases as people develop more trust, but it will always be there.

Handshakes appeared during the Middle Age as a way to show that people were not carrying any weapons.

Let's shake hands!

Currently, it's a reflex in any given networking event, which is replaced in some countries by a vow in which the inclination angle should be proportional to the interlocutor's importance – lesser angle, lesser importance.

Naturally, we might also judge our contacts by their handshakes or by their vow and, in this case, we often see that we are also being judged.

Handshakes should be vigorous and grasping the whole hand; otherwise, we might be creating a feeling of disgust, often defined as «shaking a dead person's hand».

Nevertheless, one needs to be careful with the vigor. We must consider the finesse of the hand we're shaking.

One of the most important moments while establishing contacts is cards' exchange. Nevertheless, it is a moment where, more often than not, some big mistakes are made:

A business card is not a sticker

- Hand over your card; don't be afraid and wait to be the second handing out cards.

- If you're dealing with a group, deliver the cards individually and, for that reason, always carry lots of cards around, since you never know when you'll meet a large group.

- When handing out your cards, don't be ungracious; give some importance to the card, but don't over do it.

- When receiving a card, take close attention at it, read the information and check to see if there's some information on the back.

- If when reading a card you're confronted with some doubt or if you discover a contact point, try to include this information in the conversation.

- If necessary, make notes on the card with additional information gathered during the conversation. Bear in mind that, as far as politeness goes, the best is to use the back of the card. For a Japanese person, it is really disrespectful to write on the front of the cards.

- Store the cards you receive in a card holder or in a box. This demonstrates two things: that you're both organized and respectful.

Don't smile only for the camera

Don't forget about the power of the smile. When we smile, we trigger smiles, it is contagious. We all will rather be with someone who smiles than with someone who's constantly frowning.

Be natural in your smile: don't overwork it, but take advantage of its power in all contacts you establish.

Mind not to shoot yourself in the foot

In order to communicate well, it is necessary to align our verbal and nonverbal communication skills, with the risk of making our interlocutors confused.

In various situations, people auto-sabotage themselves due to a misalignment between these two types of communication. Therefore, and during a contact please avoid:
- looking at your watch when your interlocutor is speaking;
- searching for other people while talking to someone else;
- quickly storing your contact's card without even looking at it;
- staring at your shoes when talking;
- mistaking networking with flirting;
- drinking too much;
- moving from one side to another while talking;
- gestures such as scratching continuously, biting your nails or performing nose inspections.

4

KNOWLEDGE
NETWORKS

The Importance of Knowledge Networks

There is an old expression that says «Information is power». This expression is based on a reality which humanity experienced until a couple of years ago; but information is no longer a scarce and inaccessible resource.

The 9/11 National Commissions clearly stated that there was information reporting that Al Qaeda was in fact preparing the attacks; nevertheless, they failed to be prevented; what failed here was the interpretation given to the information, i.e., to knowledge.

In this particular case, we were able to witness, quite dramatically, that information is no longer power.

Background

We live surrounded by information: Information is bought, sold, rented and given. It's difficult to imagine a time with only two TV channels, less than a dozen radio stations, newsstands with less than twenty publications and absent Web. Nevertheless, that time was a reality only twenty years ago.

The information flux is immense. I will provide you with some data to better understand how, in fact, we live in an exponential time of generating information.

- Every month, around 3 billion searches are performed on Google.
- The number of text messages sent per day is superior to the world population.
- Every day, 3000 books are published.
- In 2007, the information generated was greater than that created over the last 5000 years.
- Technical information is doubling every two years.

Power, according to its definition, comes from controlling scarce resources and information is not a scarce resource at all.

Having people and systems capable of handling this gigantic flux of information is the challenge we face and will face.

A tsunami of information

How to take so much
information in?

The big question today is not how to obtain information but rather how to digest so much information. No one, at this moment, is capable of saying that he/she knows everything there is to know about a certain area of knowledge.

My advice is to copy one successful experience: The Internet. No server contains all web pages, for lack of capacity, and so the solution was to create a global network of connected computer networks, each of them containing a minuscule piece of the immense puzzle that is the Internet. The Web, just as information, continues to grow exponentially.

Currently, even without realizing it, people are already beginning to copy that model. The problem is that it is not yet a known fact, because we still associate intelligence to memorization of information.

The coming of this paradigm shift will happen sooner or later, for lack of alternatives. We will witness the depreciation of memorization and the growing appreciation of critical thinking. This will have a great impact on global educational systems, which always put an emphasis on memorization, making it the fulcrum point of evaluation.

We live in a transition phase and those who understand the true implications behind such a shift will gain a substantial competitive advantage.

Information vs.
knowledge

It is essential to distinguish between information and knowledge. Everything captured by our senses is information, what we choose to do with that information is knowledge, something that can be shared with others, transforming it once again into knowledge.

Share!

The secret of great networkers is their generosity in sharing knowledge without immediately expecting anything in return.

Networks have a life of their own. You will see that by sharing your knowledge with someone in your network; a day, a month or a year later something will be given in return (more knowledge, a business opportunity, etc.). This is the essence of the society in which we live, more interconnected and dynamic than ever.

Don't thank your network for everything you get from it, simply because your parents taught you to say thanks after getting a present.

Express your gratitude by giving back and this will provide access to extraordinary opportunities.

Search Engines

I still remember the time when there were no such things as search engines, when the search for information on a certain entity or person was a troublesome process and when only some companies had access to quality information.

Currently, information is accessible to everyone. We only have to know which tools to use in this digital age.

Google is undoubtedly the most widely used search engine, being responsible for the vast majority of searches performed by web surfers; nevertheless, not many web surfers go beyond the search bar.

Google has in itself a world of applications that allow any normal mortal being to access more information, within a few seconds, than the information services of big companies could retrieve only ten years ago.

There are two fairly unknown tools, made available by Google, that might be extremely useful when gathering information:

• While using advanced search, it is possible to determine the existing links to a certain website, thus offering a vision of who is connected to that website.

• The language tools allow us, apart from translating a text from one of the main languages into another, to enter the address of a given website and automatically obtain a translation. It is important to realize that the quality of the translation will not be excellent, but it will be enough to get a good general idea of the contents displayed. This was extremely useful when I had to prepare a trip to Russia.

Have you googled today?

Everything we do and everything that is said about us online will leave a trace; therefore, it is important to frequently analyze our online presence. One of the easiest ways is to enter our name, between inverted commas, in the Google search and check out the results.

Immediately, this seems quite narcissistic, but it is not; our name is our personal brand and so it is very important to know what our associations are, what comments, what news, etc.

This way, we are able to control everything that is said about us, thus being able to perceive our competitive advantage and also to avoid some less fortunate incidents.

Wikipedia does not bite

Wikipedia is widely recognized as the greatest online knowledge database; notwithstanding, there are still some unfounded fears regarding its quality, since its open contents may be edited by anyone, as opposed to traditional encyclopedias.

Such fears are reflections of the lack of understanding regarding Wikipedia's functioning process – so I will name some clues in order to prevent that:

- Whenever a content is edited, the author and whoever requests that, are warned about that change and there's even the possibility of reverting to the previous version if such is seen convenient.

- Wikipedia is neutral, i.e., the contents representing opinions will be quickly eliminated.

- There is a chain of command within Wikipedia – the more valid contents you produce to Wikipedia, the more power you'll have within the community.

- Wikipedia is validated, on a daily basis, by millions of users.

- The contents made available by Wikipedia can be immediately updated, as opposed to traditional encyclopedias.

- Comparative studies with traditional encyclopedias show that there are fewer mistakes on Wikipedia.

- Finally, regardless of the Wikipedia page, you'll find the references and websites that served as the basis for its creation; that gives the user the means to cross information immediately.

For that reason, Wikipedia must be considered part of the arsenal of any given networker and it should be used to suppress gaps in our general and scientific knowledge or merely to obtain more information on people and entities.

Figure 4.1. Wikipedia, the biggest online encyclopedia (www.wikipedia.org)

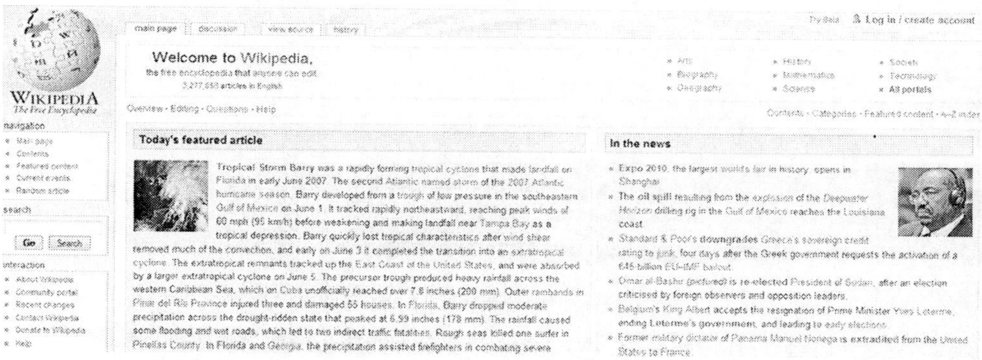

Google is a great search engine as far as word search is concerned. But it would be nice to have a specialized tool that gathered information on people, thus avoiding the feeling of looking for a needle in a haystack.

There is already such a tool, it's called Yasni, a search engine that specialises in finding every bit of online information about people. The search can be divided into different groups:

- IMAGES – pictures of the person.

- PERSONAL INFORMATION – where we can find some information such as address, through Addresses.com, or profile through MySpace or Hi5 profiles, Twitter references or videos through Blinkx.

- PROFESSIONAL INFORMATION – gathered from databases, from Wikipedia and professional networks, such as LinkedIn or Xing.

Yasni

- NEWS – gathered from Google News, Technorati, Bloglines and Google Blogs.

- PRESENCE IN OTHER WEBSITES – references to the websites that refer to that person.

- ASSOCIATED KEYWORDS – through an application called Keyword Cloud, we can quickly realize, through a visual representation, that we are linked to a person.

This search engine has an application that may be used to search for people on Facebook.

Figure 4.2. Yasni, the people search engine (www.yasni.com)

Brain searching

Search engines are extraordinary tools which allow us to sail in a sea of information. Nevertheless, they provide us with lakes of information and, consequently, how to know what is relevant, what is the correct term or even how to understand what we searched for?

For thousands and thousands of years, we grew accustomed to simply talking to someone within our network that could have some knowledge on the subject.

Figure 4.3. Aspect of the LinkedIn's advanced search tool (www.linkedin.com)

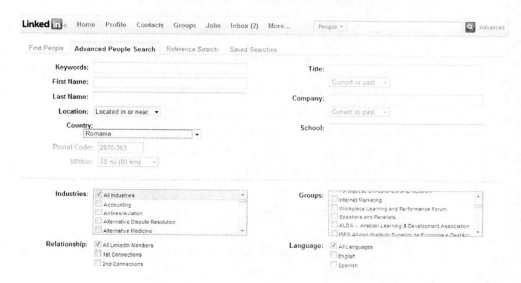

How to be Continuously Up-to-date?

The greatest challenge faced by any professional during the 21st century is the constant evolution of knowledge.

Background

Traditional methodologies for updating are not providing efficient answers and these answers will be increasingly worse, since the divergence between the need for knowledge and its production time is increasingly getting bigger.

It is necessary to use the best the Internet has to offer in order to be able to keep up with this mad race, making a preparation according to a just-in-time logic, i.e., learning when we need to learn and not learning when we don't.

Have you met TED?

Would you like to see and hear the best brains in the world sharing their discoveries on the world we live in and discussing their perspectives for the future? Then, you have to meet TED.

TED is not a person; it is an event featuring perhaps the best conferences worldwide. TED is a small non-profit organization dedicated to spreading ideas that deserve to be spread.

Everything started in a conference gathering people from three distinct worlds: Technology, Entertainment and Design (TED).

Currently, TED conferences are available for free at www.ted.com, where they can be seen:

- online, on the site;
- by downloading them to your computer;
- through the specific iTunes HD channel, which can be subscribed to and, this way, we will periodically receive new presentation to watch in our computer, iPod or iPhone.

One of TED's greatest advantages is the fact that a presentation never exceeds more than twenty minutes and, therefore you will always have time to extend your knowledge.

Figure 4.4. Excellence conferences at TED (www.ted.com)

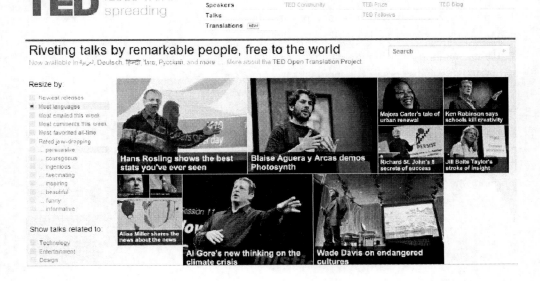

Imagine a place where you can choose any knowledge area and attend, free of costs, lectures given by professors of prestigious universities such as Berkeley, Harvard, MIT, NIH, Princeton, Stanford and Yale.

This place exists. It's called Academic Earth. It is an organization with the objective of facilitating the access to world-class contents, on a wide range of subjects that goes from Astronomy to Religion, passing through Economics, History, Entrepreneurship, and Math among others, to anyone in the world.

The best teachers at your service

Figure 4.5. Lectures from the best universities online at Academic Earth (http://academicearth.org/)

If you have ever seen me walking down the street with my headphones on, in about 90 percent of times, the chances are that I'm listening to a podcast.

With my iPod, I've learned that I have plenty of time to learn new things while walking, on public transportation, at the dentist, doing the dishes, in the car, waiting for the next flight, etc.

You have plenty of time to learn

But what is in fact a podcast? It's an audio or video recording made available online. The greatest advantage of iTunes is that it is an aggregating channel, which facilitates search according to themes and allows channel subscriptions.

Figure 4.6. Examples of podcasts available at iTunes Store (www.apple.com)

Know what the blogs are saying

Blogs are also windows to the world of experts on several knowledge areas, who use this medium to expose their views; the problem is that there are millions of blogs, so it is necessary to know how to sail through this world of information.

To achieve this, we may use a blog specialized search engine, Technorati. In June 2008, Technorati had over 113 millions blogs indexed.

Figure 4.7. Technorati, a blog search engine (http://technorati.com)

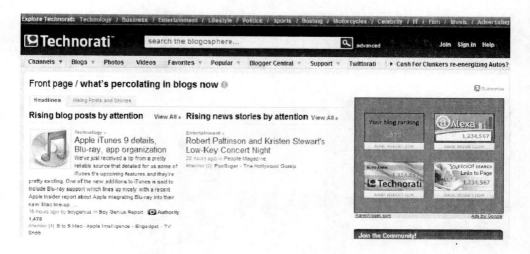

Created in 2005, YouTube is currently the largest global supplier of media content; but the fame brought some problems along: many companies don't allow their workers to access YouTube, since its use is essentially recreational.

YouTube is not just about kittens playing the piano

Nevertheless, YouTube has a considerable amount of informative and educational contents that deserve to be explored.

It also allows for the subscription of channels that we may consider of interest. Thus, whenever a new video is added to the subscribed channel, we'll be notified by email.

Figure 4.8. Example of a YouTube channel featuring advice for trainers
(www.youtube.com/user/VideoTipsforTrainers)

Create your news
agency

For a short period of time during my teenage years, I had the privilege of obtaining the weekly Portuguese newspapers through a neighbor who was a press secretary and who, after analyzing the publications, instead of throwing them away, would hand them over to me so that I could quench my curiosity on global events. In the 80s, this was indeed a privilege.

Today, this wouldn't be regarded as a privilege. Right now, by using Google Reader, it is possible to read news from everywhere in the world, made available by global and local media, websites, and blogs, making it possible to create our own news agency.

Google Reader allows us to add information from any given website, as long as it has a RSS system. The websites that want to make information available use this type of technology. Thus, it is possible to obtain information from all the subscribed websites on a single web page without having to visit each one of them.

Figure 4.9. Information aggregator Google Reader (www.google.com/reader)

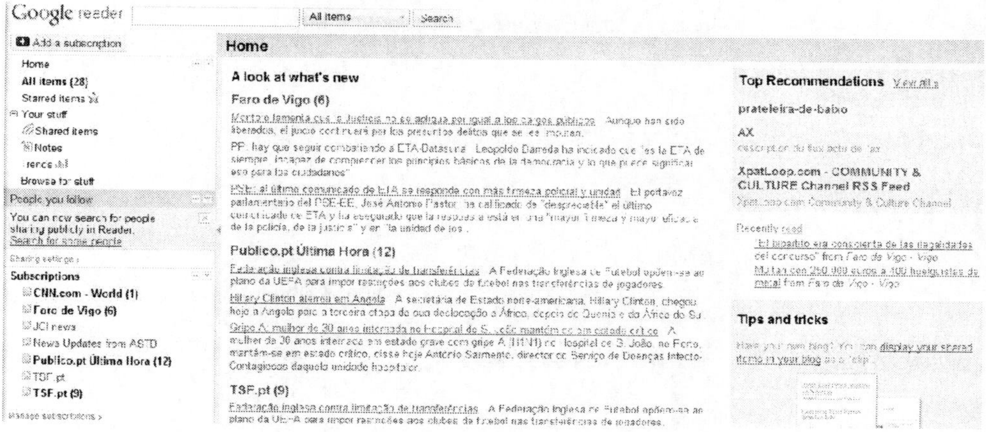

In the 1990s, I became familiar with a clipping company, whose work consisted of receiving, during the night, the next day's newspapers, taking them into a room, selecting contents according to the clients' requests and produce files of clips that would have to be available at the beginning of the next day at the largest Portuguese companies.

The extraordinary times we now live in, allow everyone to have such a service totally for free.

Through Google Alerts service, we have at our disposal the key-words to receive information through our email accounts.

It is also possible to choose:
• sources;
• news;
• blogs;
• web;
• video;
• discussion groups;
• all the options mentioned;
• send frequency;
• when checked;
• once a day;
• once a week.

Be alert, stress free

The possibilities at our disposal are infinite. We are able to follow up on our own information, on our company's, on competitors, on a particular product, a service, a concept, etc.

Figure 4.10. Google Alerts, your private clipping service (www.google.com/alerts)

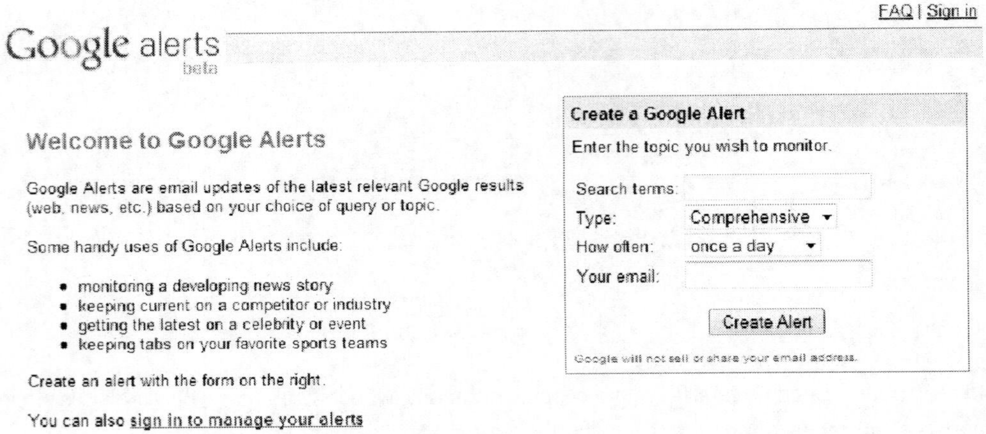

FAQ | Sign in

Google alerts
beta

Welcome to Google Alerts

Google Alerts are email updates of the latest relevant Google results (web, news, etc.) based on your choice of query or topic.

Some handy uses of Google Alerts include:

- monitoring a developing news story
- keeping current on a competitor or industry
- getting the latest on a celebrity or event
- keeping tabs on your favorite sports teams

Create an alert with the form on the right.

You can also sign in to manage your alerts

Create a Google Alert

Enter the topic you wish to monitor.

Search terms: _____
Type: Comprehensive ▾
How often: once a day   ▾
Your email: _____

Create Alert

Google will not sell or share your email address.

5

NETWORK PRESENCE

The Connected World

We live in a completely connected world and over the last four years, some powerful tools were left at our disposal. Tools that allow us to manage our networks.

Online social networks have suffered an almost spectacular growth, where millions and millions of people are joining in, – creating a real online extension for everyone.

In 1994, actor Kevin Bacon gave an interview in which he declared he had already partnered with everybody in Hollywood. Based on this interview, three students at Albright College created a game whose objective was to find out exactly how Kevin Bacon was connected to the people in the movie industry.

The authors of the game actually wrote a book, Six Degrees of Kevin Bacon, that brings us to an interesting conclusion: We all live, at the most, at six degrees of separation from any other person on Earth.

This means that we are connected with everybody and in order to establish contact. We only need to have five people introducing us in a sequence.

Nevertheless, trying to put this on paper – the real extension of our contact network and the contact networks of our contacts – is an impossible task for two reasons:

• the extension of the networks: One can easily achieve, on a third or fourth level of contact, millions of interconnected people;

• the dynamics of each individual contact: The number of contacts one has varies on a daily basis.

To answer this challenge, some professional websites (Professional Network Service) came forward, of which we will speak in greater detail in the following chapter.

Digital non-verbal
communication

In chapter 3, we discussed the fact that with the increasingly bigger growth of digital communication, it is important to adapt the way we communicate to the digital world.

When communicating in writing in the digital world, whether by email, by instant messaging, text messages or other types of services, you should bear in mind the following:

• write in a clear and direct manner;
• keep in mind the size of the screens where the message will be displayed;
• use emoticons as a way to associate emotions with the message.

Likewise, you must recognize the limitations of written communication:
• it is not suitable for delicate situations;
• it's hardly motivating;
• it breaks way to multiple interpretations.

For these reasons, we should also use audio and video communication tools, which are able to mime face-to-face communication easily.

21st century-style
communication

Thanks to the technological evolution and growing bandwidth over the last few years, audio and video communications have become something quite easy, with top-class quality.

Nevertheless, only very few people use these means in synchronised communication and fewer in asynchronised communication.

About this last subject, there are several software programs that allow us to send audio and video messages by email, but unfortunately these are not widely used.

Regarding video messages, their scarce use is less logical, since this type of communication has several advantages:
• it is faster to produce than a written message;
• it allows the association of nonverbal elements;
• the explanation of complex concepts is made easier.

Figure 5.1. ooVoo allows for the sending of video messages through email (www.oovoo.com)

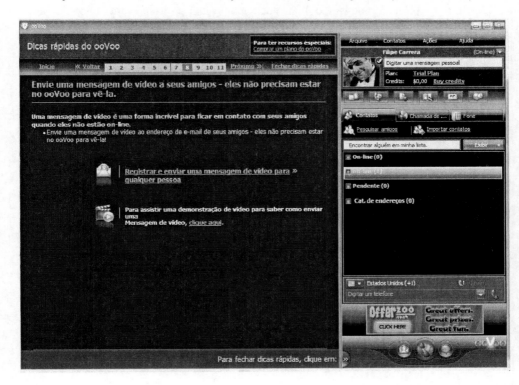

A network is not valuable for the number of contacts it holds, but rather by their quality (for instance, if you stand in the middle of the street handing out business cards, although you might obtain plenty of contacts, your network will be quite worthless).

How valuable is a network

Therefore, it is important to have a certain degree of involvement with each contact; otherwise, we will stand before a modern version of a football sticker collection.

Although it is quite difficult to say how much a network is worth, it is possible to calculate a network's worth by:
• the percentage of business originating on the network;
• the number of clients originating on the network;
• turnover rate.

There is even a website – Tweetvalue – which performs an estimate, in dollars, of how much your Twitter profile is worth, based on available information.

Figure 5.2. Tweetvalue, a website that calculates a value for your Twitter profile (http://tweetvalue.com/)

Becoming an Expert

Background

During an online lecture at MIT, famous author Thomas Friedman (http://academicearth.org/lectures/the-world-is-flat) talks about the several stages of globalization, stating that we now live in a third stage of globalization.

During stage 1.0, globalization was jump-started by several countries and Portugal played a vital role at this stage. During stage 2.0, multinational companies led the way in driving global integration, but in stage 3.0 individuals will be leading the way, because they have the means to work together, wherever they are.

Personally, not only do I agree with this, I also have put it into practice; as a person who has already been a speaker in Washington DC, in the USA, Ulan Bator in Mongolia, Vilnius in Lithuania and Mumbai in India, among other quite different spaces.

As a professional and some years ago, I stopped considering my competitors only on a local scale. Besides, I also need the global experiences to help people locally.

But how can we manage to compete within such a global market? The key is in the expertise, not like it was done a couple of years ago, when people developed some expertise in a specific area and were stuck to that professional path for the rest of their lives.

Such a commitment may be counterproductive, since we witness the appearance and disappearance of expertise fields on a daily basis. I stand for a flexible expertise in a wide sense and not in a strict sense. This allows us to change our work – field if necessary, instead of forcing ourselves to continue in a dead end.

Therefore, when choosing a theme of expertise, we must take into account some basic assumptions:
• Do we have a true calling and passion for the area?
• Are there development perspectives?
• Are there adjacent expertise areas?
• Will we be able to bring in something new?

Choosing a theme

After choosing our theme, we must align our activity and even some of our free time with that expertise.

This implies the adoption of behaviors, such as:
• Looking for specialized information in our area of expertise.
• Having one or two mentors.
• Participating in related events.
• Increasing our contact network in that particular area.
• Becoming a part of associations dedicated to our field of expertise.
• Always being up-to-date.
• Promoting ourselves as experts in our networks.

Keeping up with the theme

Creating contents

One of the most convincing ways to become recognized as an expert in a given area is achieved by creating contents and using two means of promotion:
• traditional;
• online.

Traditional broadcasting mechanisms

Traditional broadcasting mechanisms basically include:
• writing articles in newspapers and magazines
• taking part of radio and TV shows;
• speaking at conferences;
• writing books.

Traditional mechanisms have two major limitations:

• you are always depending on third parties in order to gain visibility We need someone to give us a chance to address the world.

• We address, not the audience we previously targeted, but rather the audience of the medium we use (for instance, during a television interview, our audience is made of the people who tune in to see that channel at that particular moment and not necessarily of the people we intended).

Online broadcasting mechanisms

We can use several online mechanisms to assume ourselves as experts in a given field. Here are some examples:
• publishing a blog;
• writing articles for websites;
• writing an e-book;
• making podcasts;
• uploading videos.

On this last point, I can refer to two characters, Gary Vaynerchuck and Johnny Lee, who apparently don't have anything in common except something vital, being recognized as experts in their areas – the passion for the theme they chose.

Gary Vaynerchuck was a complete stranger a few years ago. The son of the owner of a liquor shop in New Jersey, he never aligned with the elitist vision of wine connoisseurs in the USA.

He knew that there was a market of people who couldn't relate to that elite, but who, nonetheless, enjoyed good wine and were available to learn more and, ultimately, to buy more and better wine.

Gary had an immense passion for wine, but he faced a problem. During the last century this would be an insurmountable barrier for him to become an expert – he didn't like to write.

Nevertheless, Gary is a communicative and enthusiastic individual. So when he started recording 20-minute videos about wine, he instantly knew that he had found his way.

Quickly Gary became a celebrity across the USA, being invited to attend several national shows, such as Late Night with Conan O'Brien. The market considered Gary an expert and his recommendations influenced wine sales across the United States.

His videos are a landmark of what can be achieved with a simple web-cam and a website. And, now that we mention him, he's a great aficionado of Portuguese wines. Check out his videos, they are worth your time!

How about
a glass of Port?

Figure 5.3. Gary Vaynerchuck's Wine Library TV (http://tv.winelibrary.com)

Do you really know everything about Wii?

Johnny Lee is the typical shy computer guy who loves technology particularly, Wii's remote controllers. Johnny has a dream: To make technology easy and accessible to all.

While playing with his Wii, he discovered he could take console-gaming a step further. For instance by transforming any canvas into an interactive board and this only with an investment of 40 Euros, – or transforming a flat screen into a 3D screen with an additional investment of 15 Euros.

Johnny shared his discoveries with the world through YouTube. His YouTube channel has more than 14 thousand subscribers and his videos were watched more than 10 million times.

The popularity led him to be invited to one of TED's conferences in February 2008 (www.ted.com/index.php/talks/johnny_lee_demos_ wii_remote_hacks.html).

Figure 5.4. Johnny Lee's YouTube channel (www.youtube.com/user/jcl5m)

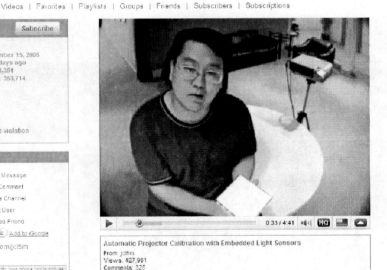

Creating an Action Plan

Reading something about networking, following some advice or creating contents – all will be quite useless without planning, visualizing the future we desire.

Never before have we had, at our disposal, so many means; therefore, we must be practical, coherent and systematic in our approach.

Our society is deeply worried about where we're heading; as a consequence, there are plenty of articles discussing how to be successful or how to become rich. However, there is little concern about determining our starting point, our market positioning.

Imagine someone blindfolded you and, a few hours later, you would find yourself in a distant corner of the world, being told that you had to return home. Your main concern would be to know where you were so that you could then establish a route back.

For several years now, I have been a host at a workshop about Self-knowledge. The workshop has already had 400 participants across 20 countries. It is based on professionally-applied SWOT (Strengths, Weaknesses, Opportunities and Threats) analysis. It is quite interesting to realize that all over the world there are people who are searching for their paths, even before they know where they are positioned.

Do this simple exercise: Take a piece of paper and a pen and list the following elements about yourself. But, during a first stage, do it on your own, don't talk to anybody else, because this will surely contaminate your analysis:

- STRENGTHS and WEAKNESSES – all of your idiosyncrasies explained on three different levels: Qualities and flaws, training and finally experience.

- OPPORTUNITIES and THREATS – everything that is out of your scope but will condition, for better or for worse, your professional path (something related to regulatory changes, consumer behavior, new technologies, new markets, etc).

After doing this list, discuss your findings with your friends, colleagues, mentors, family or other people who you think could make a good contribution to the building of a portrait of yourself.

Where do we want to go?

We have already established our market position, – and now? Here's the moment when we establish our goals.

At this stage, we must define real, measurable, ambitious goals, clearly defined over specific time. These objectives must be related to the analysis of your positioning, being therefore intertwined with the opportunities available.

At this stage, I believe in the power of visualization: Focus and visualize the future and when you have made up your goals, enjoy the feeling. You just took the first step towards their materialization.

This visualization may be mental, but you can also make a poster with your objectives and place it somewhere visible.

This type of technique allows us to align the conscious brain with the unconscious brain, since the latter works by repeating information. Let me provide you with a simple example: When you get into your car and make the decision to drive somewhere, how often, after getting to your destination, are you not able to clearly remember the route you took and how you took it? Why? Because you've programmed your brain and your conscious brain to be in perfect tune with your unconscious brain.

When we ask successful people what the reason is behind their success, we often hear words like passion, commitment, persistence, and vision.

In other words, if we really want to convince others of the validity of our ideas, we must, first of all, convince ourselves.

And do keep in mind: share your goals with the people in your networks. You will see that there are lots of people willing to help you achieve them.

For me, this is the most important part of the Self-knowledge workshop that I teach. That´s because after participants define their position and outline their objectives, they are summoned to consider which actions should be performed.

I said interesting because people find out, in the vast majority of cases, they already have their answers (my role is simply to stimulate the generation of ideas by helping other participants).

The reason is simple: Who knows better than you about your own circumstances and life experiences? Look for help within your network so that you can determine the best actions.

Just as goals, the actions to be performed must be real and a clear commitment must be made towards them.

How to get there?

We have a position, we have goals and we have actions; therefore, don't lose the paper where you outlined your action plan; analyze it frequently, get a coach or a mentor to help you in following and adjusting your plan.

During the plan's follow-up, if necessary, refurbish some of your goals and actions to perform. Your plan must be flexible, adaptable to circumstances and able to use the power of your networks.

Follow-up
on your plan

6

THE POWER
OF SOCIAL MEDIA

Professional Social Networking

Professional social networking sites are changing the way we manage our networks, because each one of us is responsible for what is made available online, just like our profile.

Potential clients, suppliers, partners and recruitment companies use these sites increasingly to find the right person for the right job.

Ten years ago, I still had to convince those in charge of companies of the need to create their own site, making information on products and services available. Today, I no longer need to convince anyone of the need to have online presence, with an exception: Professionals. Many of them still consider that exposing their professional profile online will be an invasion of their privacy.

I gladly see that fewer people think like this and I can assure you that the rest will learn the hard way – by feeling excluded. Unfortunately, one of the best ways of learning is by making mistakes and dealing with the consequences.

Don't waste time if you don't have it. Create your profile on a social networking site and keep it up-to-date, because that will be your professional passport for this century.

The best known function of this type of website is related to the exposure of our professional profile before an audience of professionals and this will most certainly kill paper CVs for good.

Traditional CVs are almost a secret statement that is not validated by third parties, whereas a profile on such sites is public and can be recommended by clearly identified people.

Nevertheless, the most revolutionary function is allowing the partial solution of the six degrees of separation issue. To better understand this function, I will take my own LinkedIn network as an example.

On the next image, we see that I have 1,255 first-degree contacts. These are the contacts of people that, in a given moment, were a part of my life, because I don't accept strangers, thus adding more value to my network. These 1,255 contacts have 184,700 contacts, which in turn have 7,147,300 contacts. My LinkedIn network has a total of 7,289,900 contacts.

Furthermore, even if I don't add any more contacts, my network will still continue to grow at a rate of two thousand contacts per day, because someone on my network will add contacts and thus enrich my network.

Like so, I have a quick access to more than 4 million professionals who may help me find information, work, business, etc.

Figure 6.1. Example of a contact network at LinkedIn (www.linkedin.com)

Your Network of Trusted Professionals

You are at the center of your network. Your connections can introduce you to 7,289,900+ professionals — here's how your network breaks down:

1	**Your Connections** Your trusted friends and colleagues	**1,255**
2	**Two degrees away** Friends of friends; each connected to one of your connections	**184,000+**
3	**Three degrees away** Reach these users through a friend and one of their friends	**7,104,600+**
	Total users you can contact through an Introduction	**7,289,900+**

Linkedin

LinkedIn was first launched on May 2003, being one of the first sites of its kind, which allowed it to reach in August 2009 more than 44 million members across 200 countries and territories and 170 industries.

Any person can become a member of this community by going directly to the website or by receiving an invitation from another member.

By becoming a member, you create a profile that summarizes your professional life and training path and, from that moment on, you can invite other contacts to become a part of your network.

Through LinkedIn, you are able to:

• Manage the information made available on your public profile through your computer or wireless mobile devices.

- Introduce yourself and be introduced to potential clients, partners, employers, suppliers and experts on different subjects.

- Create and collaborate on projects, by collecting data, sharing files and solving problems.

- Be found for business or job opportunities.

- Have new information through discussions in private groups of LinkedIn members.

- Discover connections that might help you find jobs or close deals.

- Place jobs offers, with the objective of finding the best talents.

- Inform the network about what you are doing at that moment through a micro blogging function.

Personally, I use this site with some frequency to accomplish all of the above mentioned functions, saving some time and money. But the most important thing is that now it is much easier and faster to find the right person. This type of site is increasingly more readily visible to recruiters and this does not happen by chance.

Figure 6.2. LinkedIn, the largest social networking site (www.linkedin.com)

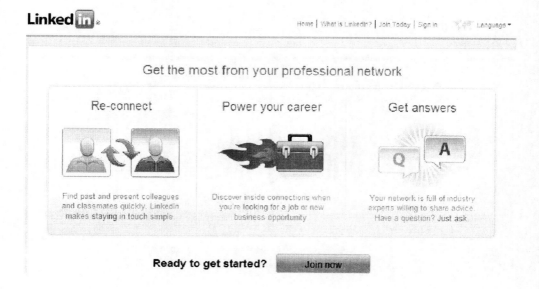

XING

Xing appeared in November 2003 in Germany, under the name Open BC/Open Business Club. In November 2006, it changed to its current name.

The growth of this network is partly due to the acquisition of other networks in Spain and Turkey. In August 2009 more than 8 million members were already part of this community, spread across 200 countries.

The available functions are quite similar to those on LinkedIn, but they feature greater technological motivations, facilitating the interconnection with personal databases, such as Microsoft Outlook contacts.

What really distinguishes XING from other platforms is its Ambassador program, available for each city or region with a significant number of members.

These ambassadors are network members that promote local events to encourage social networking as a business tool, thus enabling the sharing of ideas while people get to know each other personally.

Figure 6.3. XING social network (www.xing.com)

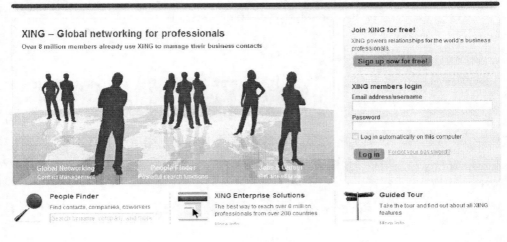

Plaxo was created on November 2002 as an online address service, allowing their users never to lose their contacts due to a computer glitch.

Plaxo

Gradually, it started to include social networking functions, to such an extent that the free Microsoft Outlook contact synchronization feature became, as of July 2009, a paid service.

In May 2009, this service already had more than 20 million members.

Figure 6.4. Plaxo network (www.plaxo.com)

The Star Tracker is a social network that tries to connect Portuguese talents across the world. To access this network, you need to be invited by another member.

The Star Tracker

It includes the normal features on this type of platforms with some interesting innovations, such as the geographical location of talents and the use of tags (specific keywords) to quickly characterize people and groups.

This network has promoted events in several world cities, where Portuguese talents are currently working.

Figure 6.5. Portuguese talents' network – The Star Tracker (www.thestartracker.com)

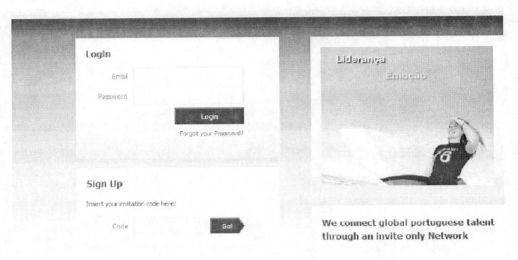

| Choosing the right network | There are plenty of other professional social networks (such as Talkbiznow, Ryze, Meet the Boss, Naymz and the Portuguese PBLink) and many others will surely appear, incorporating or not with the existing ones. |

In several seminars, I have participants deeply convinced of the importance of belonging to such networks, but they soon become overwhelmed by the number of available networks and by the effort it takes to have professional information up-to-date across all of them.

In truth, we cannot spend 80 percent of our time working on social networking sites, under the penalty of failing to do our job. Thus, here are some pieces of advice:

• Choose one main social network and keep your information updated constantly.

• Use two or three secondary social networks, place a basic profile that doesn't need constant maintenance.

• Concentrate almost all of your networking efforts on the main network.

- Ask the members of your main network to provide some advice.
- If you have a webpage, create a link for your online profile within your main network.

And how to choose your main social network? The best thing to do is to bet all your money on the largest network and to test two of them for a couple of months to see which one:

- has functions that are more appropriate for your line of business;
- has more interesting persons as members;
- allows you to obtain better results as far as contacts, information and business go.

I don´t want to end this point on professional social networking without enticing you, dear reader, to take it a step further than placing your profile online. Take advantage of the features that allow you to create sub-groups of contacts around a country, a theme, a product, a concept, etc.

Creating Sub-groups

This is an excellent way to find new contacts and to become a true expert on a given matter within a community.

Personal Social Networking

In 1995, my first email address and webpage were provided by the first global virtual community – Geocities – which allowed users to create their online presence and to be contacted through a customized email address.

Background

This type of service also allowed for the interaction between members through chat rooms. I spent loads of hours in conversations with people from every corner of the world, which I didn't know and never knew, that shared with me the same motivation to find exactly where and how far this new means could take us.

In 2003, in Australia, the first social networking site appeared, obeying Web 2.0 logic – called Friendster. This site has currently more than 100 million users worldwide, mainly in Asia.

2003 also witnessed the appearance of MySpace and Bebo; in the following year, Facebook came forward. The concept of social networking was implemented.

From 2007 onwards, there was a true explosion of these networks and Barack Obama's campaign is an excellent example of that fact having achieved record campaign donations due to the use of social networks for recruiting volunteers, supporters and contributors.

Figure 6.6. Social network Friendster (www.friendster.com)

How does it work?

When I mention social network, there is always the issue of alienating users, who spend more time in front of the computer than talking to people face to face.

This question originated due to a conceptual error. These networks do not substitute face-to-face interaction. They should be seen as an extension of our life, as a way to keep more relationships, by reinforcing them, because the basis for all good relationships is knowledge at both ends.

In this sense, these networks offer wide possibilities to deepen relationships and also have the following functions:

• online placement of profile, which includes general professional and personal information;

• updating the information on the profile through services quite similar to blogs;

• creation of networks of friends;

• sharing photographs or video albums;

• information regarding what you're doing at a specific moment;

• sending messages to other members;

• creation of thematic sub-groups;

• event organization;

• promotion of products and services;

• use of applications that improve the interactivity between users, such as questionnaires, quizzes, games, etc.

These networks are vitally important to establish relationships, to promote products, services and events, that are essential tools of modern networkers, so it is important to know some meaningful examples of these types of networks.

Facebook

In 2004, a group of students at Harvard University decided to create an exclusive network for students at that university, rapidly expanding it to other universities within the Boston area and finally to people over the age of 13.

Here are some numbers about Facebook as of August 2009:
• 250 million active users;
• 120 million access this network at least once a day;
• 30 million update their statuses at least once a day;
• 120 is the average number of contacts per user;
• 1000 million photos are uploaded per month;
• 10 million videos are uploaded per month;
• 1000 million contents (links, news, posts, notes, etc.) are shared per week;

- 2,5 million events are created per month;
- 45 million groups of users;
- 30 million access Facebook through mobile devices;
- 8 million new Facebook pages' fans per day;
- 50 languages available;
- 70 percent of users live outside the USA.

Facebook has become an extraordinary case of success and, in 2009; it became the greatest social network on the world.

More and more professionals and companies are using Facebook to promote their products and services, through ads or pages, where members can be invited to become fans.

Figure 6.7. Example of the Facebook page created about the Digital Marketing at the 2.0 Version book (www.facebook.com)

Hi5

Created a year earlier than Facebook, this social network has con-quered over 60 million users, being quite strong in Spanish-speaking Latin countries and countries such as Romania, Nepal, Tunisia, Mongolia and Portugal.

In Portugal, younger users are taking the lead; notwithstanding, websites including Facebook and MySpace are beginning to dispute the national market leadership.

Figure 6.8. Hi5, a popular social network in Portugal (www.hi5.com)

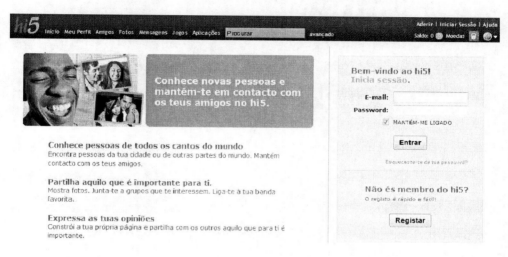

There isn't a single garage band –worthy of that name – without a MySpace page, because this is a new distribution means for music and concert promotion.

MySpace is much more than a social network of musicians, but, by allowing an easy presence to many musicians, it attracts a younger audience to the network. Up until 2009, it had taken the lead, with more than 250 million members worldwide.

MySpace has created several local versions, including one in Portugal.

MySpace

Figure 6.9. MySpace's Portuguese version, one of the largest social networks worldwide
(http://pt.myspace.com)

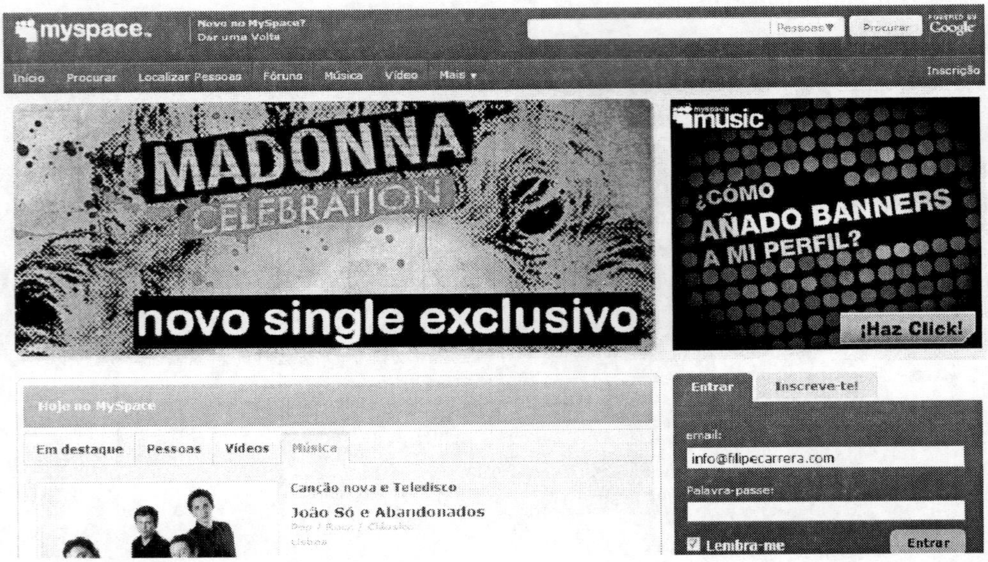

Adult Friend Finder

A living proof that the Internet acts increasingly more as an extension of our personal life is the social network AdultFriendFinder, directed at meeting intimate partners across the world, with suggestions made according to one's location.

In a world where time is an increasingly scarce resource and where professional careers are highly demanding, many people use these websites to quickly meet partners who share the same tastes, fetishes or sexual orientation.

In this type of website, the interaction is made through the platform, before a face-to-face contact, which allows people to filter efficiently and safely, thus avoiding disappointments.

AdultFriendFinder now has a total of 20 million members across the world and is ranked as the 60th most visited website on the Internet.

Figure 6.10. AdultFriendFinder, a social network dedicated to meeting sexual partners
(www.adultfriendfinder.com)

The aforementioned examples are only a small fraction of the existing social networks. As an example, the following table introduces
other relevant networks on the world.

Others

Network	Focus	Members	Website
Baboo	General	37 million	www.baboo.com
Bebo	General	40 million	www.bebo.com
Buzznet	Music	10 million	www.buzznet.com
Classmates	Former classmates	50 million	www.classmates.com
Flixter	Films	63 million	www.flixter.com
Flickr	Photo sharing	32 million	www.flickr.com
Friendster	General	90 million	www.friendster.com
Geni	Genealogy	15 million	www.geni.com
Habbo	General, for teenagers	117 million	www.habbo.com
LiveJournal	Blogs	43 million	www.livejournal.com
MyLife	Locating friends	51 million	www.mylife.com
Netlog	General	50 million	www.netlog.com
Orkut	General	67 million	www.orkut.com
Windows Live Spaces	Blogs	120 million	http://home.spaces.live.com

Publishing Contents

Background

Apart from social networks which we analyzed in the previous paragraphs, there are many other alternatives to communicate and increase our number of contacts.

What we need to realize is what the available alternatives are and to understand that, regardless of the one we choose, we should maintain the information up-to-date and coherent. Therefore, we should ask the following questions:

• Who are we trying to reach?

• What messages do we want to convey?

• How much available time do we have?

Do note that I didn't need to mention financial resources, since whatever the alternative, costs are either zero or quite miniscule – our commitment is our biggest investment.

In 2003, I was invited as a speaker to a conference on training and human resource development in Brazil. During the event, I had the chance to see that, much like in the USA, the trainers used, among other things, personal websites as a self-promotion mechanism.

When I got home, I decided to move the website I had to a more professional one, using my name as a domain, thus abandoning the pages I had created through a virtual community.

I must confess that I saw many colleagues grinning whenever I told them that I had my entire professional information on a website and often they went as far as saying: «Very interesting, but could you send me a CV by email?»

Fortunately, today, my website works as a curriculum vitae, as a window to my courses, a space enabling the interaction between clients and potential clients and an aggregator of the information I have scattered among social networks.

This means that what in 2003 was considered an interesting curiosity has become, slowly and gradually, an indispensable tool in my relationship with the market that has given me work across forty countries in four continents.

Having a personal website

Figure 6.11 Example of a personal website (www.filipecarrera.com)

Having a blog?   A blog is a type of website that allows the author to easily maintain an up-to-date presence on the Internet, since the author only has to be slightly familiar with computer skills.

Blogs work as a public journal that allows comments to be posted.

There are several websites that allow you to create a blog in an easy and free of costs way:

- Blogger: www.blogger.com;
- Blog.com: www.blog.com;
- Wordpress: www.wordpress.com;
- Toughts.com: www.thoughts.com;
- Sapo.pt: http://blogs.sapo.pt/.

Figure 6.12 Author's blog (http://filipecarrera.blogspot.com)

RSS means Really Simple Syndication and it is a technology that allows web surfers to subscribe to several sites supplying RSS feed. These typically include websites that change contents regularly.

For that reason, RSS feeds are used, to receive updated information. Thus, the user can still remain informed of several updating processes, across different sites, without needing to visit them one by one.

Therefore, many sites and blogs enable the subscription of RSS feeds, thus their use is highly recommended.

RSS

Figure 6.13. RSS logo

For 99.9% of people, Wikipedia is a means of obtaining information. Nevertheless, taking part in its construction may be a way to be identified as an expert in a given area.

Wikipedia

In order to make that happen, you can:

• create your own Wikipedia page;

• edit Wikipedia pages, taking advantage of your knowledge;

• create new Wikipedia pages on subjects you master and are still not featured in this encyclopedia;

• add links in articles to your pages that feature additional resources, such as texts, videos, files, etc.

But keep in mind that while contributing to Wikipedia, you must know the code of conduct in force:

• Do not copy the total content of an article in a different source.

• Do not delete, but rather correct and add.

• Do not use it for self-promotion.

• Do not give opinions (Wikipedia's contents are based on the principle of neutrality).

• Avoid using jargon.

• Do not sign your articles.

Figure 6.14. Wikipedia page on Eduardo Catroga (www.wikipedia.org)

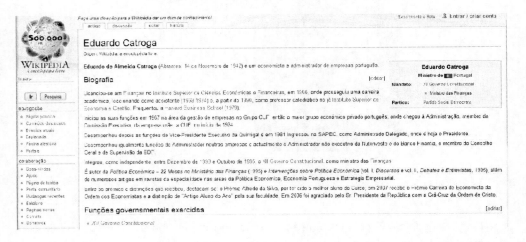

Ning

Although social networks are out there across the entire world, you have the possibility to create your own social network through Ning (www.ning.com), where you will be able to gather people who share your interest. Furthermore, this platform allows you to:

• Interact with members.
• Share contents with different formats.
• Organize events.
• Stimulate discussion.
• Etc.

Since it is a preformatted platform, it is quite simple for someone to create his/her own community. However, the hardest part is maintaining it, so your first concern should be how you'll promote it in the future.

Construct your community around a theme you feel really passionate about (it may be a hobby, a sport), since it does not mandatorily have to be related to your professional area, because, as I mentioned before, we're dealing with ways to expand your network, to go much further than your natural network.

Figure 6.15. Social network created by the author on Ning around Digital Marketing (http://dmarketing.ning.com)

Sharing Media Contents

Background

The general use of bandwidth is changing the behaviors of web surfers. From mere readers of contents splattered on a computer screen, they became researchers of media contents, not only within the computer scope but also in other devices, such as portable MP3 and MP4 players.

On the other hand, what's the best way to meet a professional? Through a set of texts or through a multimedia approach, where we can analyze photos, recordings, videos and audio files?

If we don't use these means by now, it is important to start experimenting and to learn how to use them, thus gaining new skills which will certainly be useful on the medium run, because I believe, in the same way it is important for professionals to master room presentation techniques, it will also be very important to master multimedia presentation techniques and very soon.

We live, of course, in a multimedia world and we failed to transfer that component online for two main reasons:

- Bandwidth (problem solved).

- Mental barriers, which still need to be solved (but let's see how we can break them).

Breaking through
mental barriers

But if we can only associate advantages with the use of multimedia means in conveying our message, why is that the exception and not the rule?

In my opinion, this has chiefly to do with mental barriers:

- A video is too much work and pricy – Currently, it is really very easy to create a video; the software can be found for free, digital cameras have never been cheaper and, if we wish, we can even use a mobile phone or a webcam. For this reason, creating a video is accessible to everyone as you can easily see on YouTube.

- To create multimedia content, we need professional actors – this mental barrier is related to a comparison term. It is quite interesting to see professionals, who are at great ease in conveying knowledge to their peers, become intimidated when a camera starts rolling. The big problem here is attempting to imitate actors or anchorpersons. Regarding a product's use, the most important thing is not to have a famous actor explaining how to use the product, but rather someone who, while not an actor, is able at any given moment to provide support to customers through video explanation, which will be registered on the product's page, so that in the future other clients will also be able to access it.

• It is faster to type a text than elaborating multimedia content – a well-written, broad and motivating text takes incomparably longer to be achieved than a multimedia presentation. A text in written language demands much higher care and one needs to be constantly thinking about the circumstances in which it will be read.

These barriers will seem even more absurd when our communications start to use more image than they use now, because we still see voice recording and video as something only actors are allowed to do, as opposed to regular human beings.

So how can we start to put multimedia contents online right away? Quite simply!

Necessary equipment:

• Digital camera, mobile phone with camera or webcam.

• Computer with microphone.

• A support to place the produced contents: web server, hard drive, CD, DVD or memory card.

Inexpensive suggestion of software programs that create multimedia contents:

• Video production on Windows – you can use Windows Movie Maker, which is already a part of Windows operating system.

• Screen capture and audio and video recording – several free programs may be used, such as CamStudio (www.redersoftware.com), or paid programs such as Camtasia Studio (www.techsmith.com) or Captivate (www.adobe.com). It is also possible with these programs to perform online PowerPoint based commercial presentations.

Practical advice to start right away!

In a nutshell, there are no objective reasons not to change and it is important to start experimenting in order to further adequate communication to the needs of the receivers, – by creating the habit of avoiding frequent email conversations between professionals and customers, which take an unnecessarily long time to obtain unsatisfactory results.

Next, some online services that facilitate the uploading of multimedia contents.

Slideshare

You prepared a wonderful PowerPoint presentation but only 10 people had the chance to see it? Slideshare is a service that may become your channel to reach a wider audience.

Through this service, you can easily take your Word or PowerPoint presentations and place them at everyone's disposal. Presentations may include sound and video, particularly through YouTube.

Figure 6.16. Slideshare, a presentation sharing service (www.slideshare.com)

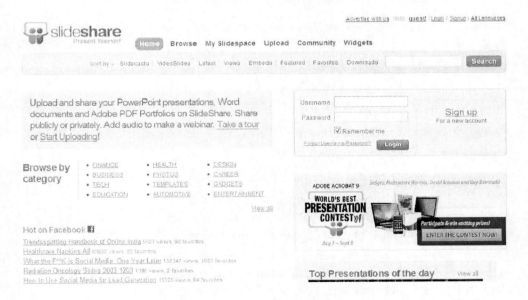

Uploading presentations may serve various purposes, for instance:

• Promoting a product or service.

• Showing the highlights of your professional experience.

• Solving clients and potential clients' doubts.

• Showing your design, photography and presentations' conception skills.

Currently, it is possible to integrate Slideshare in your Facebook, LinkedIn and Xing profile, allowing the visualization of presentations that you consider relevant directly in your profile.

The term podcast was first used in 2004, by conjugating the words Pod (MP4 player) and broadcast. The author of podcasts is called a podcaster.

Podcasts

A podcast is a series of digital media files (either audio or video) that are released episodically or periodically and can be downloaded through a website or a podcatcher (iTunes, Zune, Juice or Wimap).

These programs allow you to download these media files unto your computer or MP3 and MP4 players, so you can listen and watch while offline, which is particularly useful during travels or when you're in a place with limited Internet access.

In the USA, podcasts are much more popular than in Europe, probably because there is a habit of buying audio books.

In Portugal, podcasting is an exception, according to my point of view, because of the type of contents we are used to hearing on the radio, where music plays a predominant role.

Nevertheless, this is not a reason for not using podcasts to promote our work, our ideas or wishes. The most important thing is to determine if your target market will hear you. And the only sure way to know that is by trying.

By using a website such as MyPodcast and a computer with a microphone, you can:

• Use the client program, supplied by the website that allows you to create a podcast, and to upload it to the MyPodcast website, as if it was a video blog.

• Keep in mind that the visitors to your MyPodcast page may subscribe to your podcasts and receive them as you publish them in
iTunes, Google Homepage, Google Reader, MyYahoo or other
podcatchers.

Try it and you will see that in less than 5 minutes you have your own
audioblog.

Figure 6.17. MyPodcast allows the creation and distribution of podcasts (www.mypodcast.com)

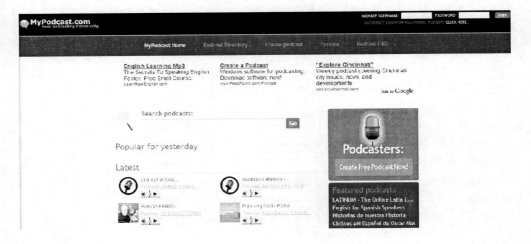

You.TV

As we have already seen, YouTube is much more than a place where
we can see cats playing the piano. It can be and should be your window to the world.

Currently, with a webcam or a digital webcam (some are already prepared for YouTube), you can easily upload video files.

Although this might be easy, you should bear in mind some issues
while producing your videos:

• The sound should be audible. Avoid exterior sets or big rooms if
you don't have a microphone.

• You may eliminate the original soundtrack and narrate over it, if
this is more convenient.

- Keep light in mind: Don't shoot against the light or next to the light, because you can be occulted by shadow.

- Check to see if the set and the clothes you're wearing are aligned with the image you're trying to convey.

- Be natural: Don't try to imitate someone you saw on television.

- Add subtitles or balloons to identify people, objects or locations. YouTube gives you the possibility to add these elements to your video.

Figure 6.18 Author's channel on Informal Training (www.youtube.com/InformalTraining)

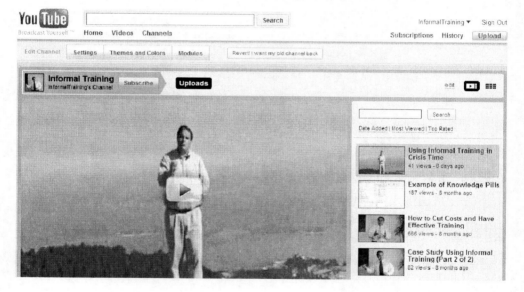

While producing, don't forget to:

- Start off by personalizing the YouTube channel you're using. You may perform a simple customization, using models available at the website.

- be sensible about titles, descriptions and tags (key-words) related to the channel.

- give proper titles to the videos.

- make a description that helps viewers understand what the video is about even before watching it.

- add precise tags (key-words) in the video's description, thus making the life of the people searching for your contents a little easier.

- use connection options to Twitter and Facebook, so that your followers and friends are able to know immediately that you´ve published a new video.

Viddler

Placing videos online is not a YouTube's exclusive feature; there are other sites sharing the same functions.

Viddler may be used as an alternative or complementary means to YouTube.

This service, although not so popular, allows for the easy publication in other channels, including iTunes, which, in its turn, has the enormous advantage of allowing their users to see contents, even if offline.

Figure 6.19. Viddler, a service to publish videos online (www.viddler.com)

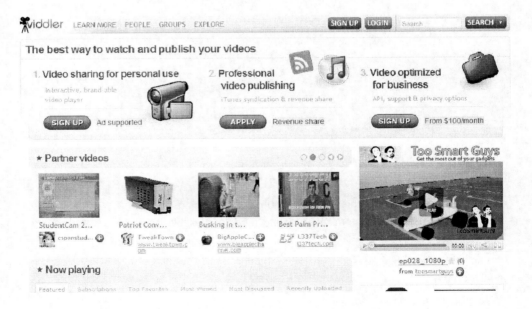

In case you are wondering «I'd rather place my videos on YouTube because if I do no one will be able to download my videos», think again. There are several programs that work as browser plug-ins that allow users to store videos on any computer.

The only sure way to protect your multimedia contents is to place subtitles and audio features that clearly indicate their origin. Thus, even if someone uses them without your permission, he/she will always be promoting you.

Today, there are numerous sites accepting online video publishing and some even provide reports on the number of visitors of the pages containing the videos and about the videos being watched.

Considering that we should not overlook any service, the time spent publishing videos across several networks (YouTube, Yahoo, MySpace, Blip.tv, Viddler, Twitter, Facebook, etc.) will surely exceed your production time, without mentioning the time we would have to invest in analyzing reports from each website.

Tubemogul

Figure 6.20. Tubemogul, online video distribution service (www.tubermogul.com)

Tubemogul appears to avoid unnecessary loss of time that allows for the publication of an online video in up to 20 different networks. This provides access to reports of different networks in a simple document, thus enabling comparisons.

Even if the videos haven't been uploaded through Tubemogul, it is possible to receive reports comparing the views of videos placed across different networks.

Microblogging

Background

For the past two years, we've witnessed a Twitter «fever» which quickly spread across social networks. Right now, it is possible to describe what you're doing through micro blogging.

It is called micro blogging because it is almost like keeping a journal in a few words and, in some cases, with the possibility to add photographs, videos or presentations.

And the more we share what we do, the more we will want to share (sometimes even sharing too much).

At this point, I can't resist recalling an episode that happened to me last June. During a conference in Budapest, a Romanian colleague and I accompanied a beautiful colleague to the hotel after a party. Although he showed great interest in her, he seemed even more interested in tweeting to followers about the details of the party. Result: He had no luck!

I confess that I am a moderate Twitter user. I prefer to update my status on Facebook or LinkedIn. Nevertheless, I have tried to intensify my use, thanks to sites that are directly connected to Twitter, such as Facebook, YouTube, Seesmic, among others.

For instance, during the production of this book, I shared the fact with my network that I was writing. – and, sometimes, how my work was progressing, thus obtaining encouraging words and contributes from around the world (refer to Chapter 8).

Twitter is the most famous micro blogging service. It enables its users
to send and read messages up to 140 characters, which can be sent
via the Twitter website, external applications or SMS (the latter depends on availability at the telecommunications operator).

Do you tweet?

This service, created in 2006, has known an extraordinary growth
over the last two years. It is now considered to be the third most used
social network with more than 55 million monthly visitors.

Apart from having influenced the behavior of other social networks,
Twitter has created a new communication space that reports events
while they're happening (whether it's a party in Budapest or a rebel-
lion against the electoral result in Tehran).

Figure 6.21. Twitter, the most famous micro blogging service (http://twitter.com)

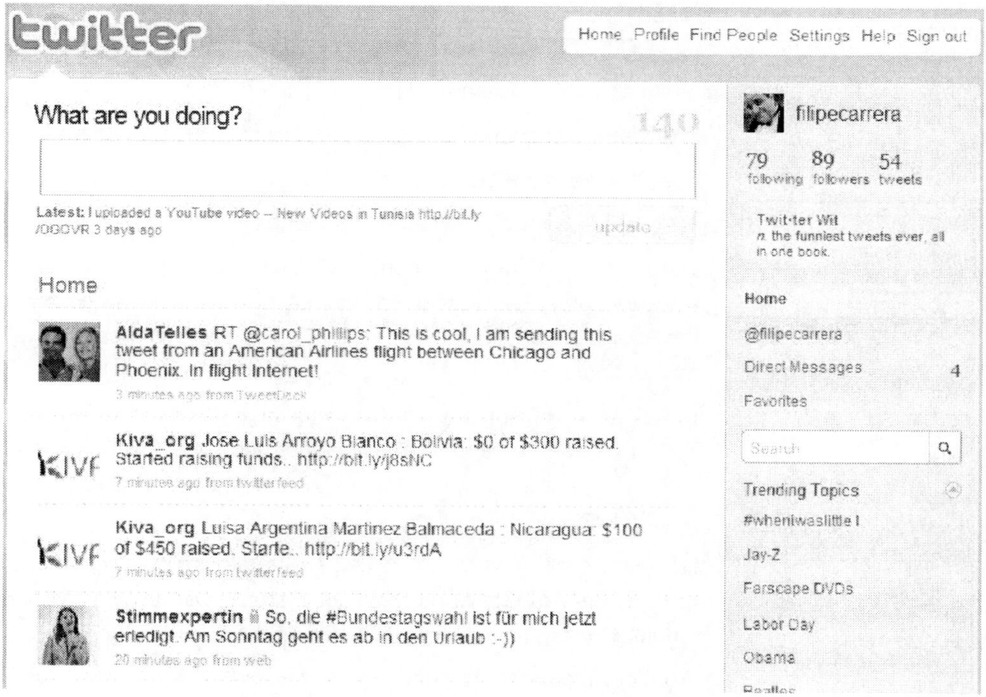

Thanks to Twitter, anonymous citizens can now cause a deeper and
faster impact on their communities, – even more than the media is
able to compose the news. The fact that the media are now starting

to monitor Twitter does not happen at random and it is quite similar to what happened a couple of years ago when they started using data from blogs.

Twitter is, for several reasons and in many ways, of extreme importance to networkers, to:

- Gather recent information on people, products, services, companies, industries, etc.

- Disclose information about what you're doing. This can be disclosed once more by other users.

- Create opportunities to meet your followers by tracking their location.

Speaking Twitter

Although Twitter is quite simple and accessible for all users, it has developed a number of terms that we need to know:

- Following: It means that we are receiving messages from someone, i.e., we're following a user.

- Follower: Person who accompanies a user.

- Tweet: A message published on Twitter.

- Tweetering: Sending messages on Twitter.

- @user: a public reply to someone else's twitter message. Thus, whoever sees the message knows that it is an answer to a user. If the user uses applications such as Tweetdeck, this message will be highlighted.

- DM (Direct Message): A private message exchanged between Twitter users. These messages will not appear at Twitter's public area or search. This type of messages can only be made between people following each other.

- RT (Retweet): A way to broadcast interesting messages from other users. Normally, the message's shape will be «RT @user: Original message, many times including a link».

- Trending Topics: Most mentioned topics. On the right side of Twitter, we can see the 10 most mentioned topics at the moment by the user in their messages. This allows us to understand immediately what is going on.

- Hashtag (#) – there is not a system for classifying tweets; therefore, users created #, a symbol that should proceed the term describing the reason behind our message (for instance, #Elections). This will facilitate searches and, at the same time, will increase the possibilities of appearing on the 10 most mentioned topics.

- Tweetup – an organized or impromptu gathering of people that use Twitter, arranged via Twitter.

- Tiny URL – with only 140 characters available, it is quite hard to send certain web addresses; therefore, when we see tweets, we see small and weird web addresses (URL), but if we click them, we're directed to the right pages. This is performed by Twitter's URL shortening services or other websites.

Twitter is an excellent space to build relations; thus, we should bear in mind the following assumptions:

- Be clearly identified.

- Read the comments on your company, brand and product regularly – and be prepared to answer back, both to good and mad remarks.

- Use a friendly and informal tone in your message.

- Answer questions directed at you.

- If a message is interesting, resend it (RT). Sharing of ideas is highly appreciated on this community.

- Place links to articles and websites that you think your followers might enjoy even if not related to your area of business.

- Don't use inadequate language or SPAM.

- Try to make your messages valuable to your followers.

Become a Twitter Pro

Ping.fm is a tool I love, just as I love any other tool that helps me communicate better and help me save time.

By diving into the world of micro blogging, I started updating my status in all the social networks I subscribe to. Whenever I needed to update my status, I would keep my browser open with several tabs and I would update on one particular network and quickly copy paste into the others. Thus, I thought I was very clever because I could update my status in about 3 or 4 minutes.

Being quicker than your own shadow

Such feeling changed when I saw Ping.fm. On this website, by simply entering my status, it automatically updates all social networks and instant messaging programs, such as Microsoft Messenger and Skype. Now, it only takes a few seconds to update my status on all the networks I participate in.

Ping.fm has developed many ways through which I don't even need to visit the website to update my status, namely:

• A tool bar as a Firefox, Safari or Internet Explorer plug-in.

• SMS (users outside of the USA and Canada have to text a United Kingdom number).

• Email (for an email address specifically created for each user).

Figure 6.22. Ping.fm allows you to update your status in all your social networks (http://ping.fm)

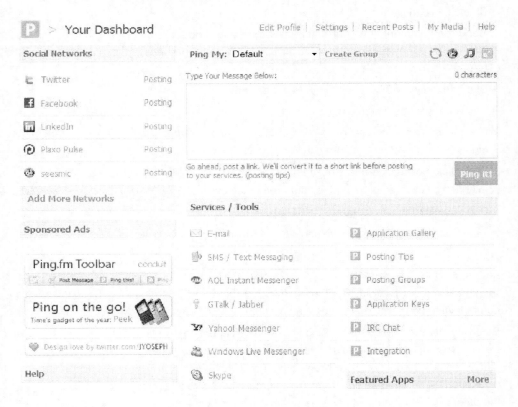

Tweetdeck is a Twitter application for your computer's desktop which, as similar applications, allows users to send and receive messages on Twitter and Facebook directly in your desktop without having to visit the websites.

By working directly on our computer, we immediately know, through a visual or sound notification, that our Facebook, MySpace and Twitter contacts have updated their status or sent new messages.

Here's a very interesting application if we need to follow what's happening in real time. If we don't, it can become a distraction.

Personally, I use it now and then, but I think it's quite useful, particularly during those moments when you need to study the effects of a promotional action, using social networks, since it's a fast way to easily obtain comments and feedback in your networks.

Tweetdeck

Figure 6.23. TweetDeck, an application to organize micro blogging (http://tweetdeck.com)

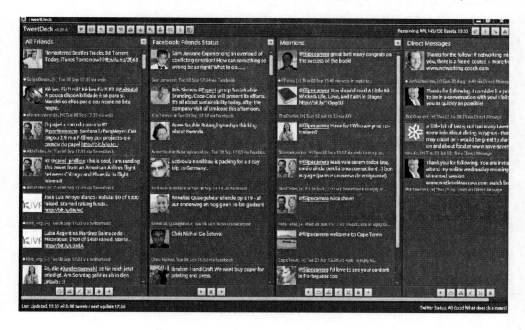

Seesmic

Seesmic, known as «video Twitter», allows users to create video messages by uploading videos or direct recording with a webcam.

Due to the technology in use, it is much easier to record and publish a video message in this community that can be automatically shared on Twitter. For that purpose, Seesmic sends a message to our Twitter account with a tiny url, in order to obey the 140 character limit imposed by Twitter.

In micro blogging, video is a good way to acquire a new competence – speaking to a camera. Therefore, give it a try!

Seesmic also provides a desktop application, quite similar to TweetDeck.

Figure 6.24. Seesmic, «Video Twitter» (http://seesmic.tv)

7

WORKING ON THE NET

And Now... Web 2.0!

If, at the end of the 18th century, we were to ask a local from Manchester of his opinion about the Industrial Revolution, he would probably just stand there staring at us without a faint clue of what we were talking about. The term Industrial Revolution was only coined around 1830, fifty years after its beginning.

An historical period is only identified as a fast changing period when seen in the future and during that particular moment you can only make guesses about what's going on.

I would say that what's been happening for the last four years has no precedent in the history of mankind. For the first time, the construction of commercial, friendship and even love relationships is not conditioned by space and time.

Throughout this chapter, I will put forward some evidence of that unprecedented revolution in our behavior, while being aware of that, as during the Industrial Revolution, this is an asymmetrical movement with some consequences already being suffered, whereas other consequences still aren't felt. But they soon will be.

The Revolution we are living is called Web 2.0.

Web 2.0 is a term coined in 2004 by American company O'Reilly Media to designate a second generation of online-based communities and services, such as wikis and application-based social networks.

Although the term has a connotation that might indicate a new Internet version, it does not refer to an update made to any technical specifications but rather to cumulative changes in the ways users see the Web.

But what distinguishes Web 2.0, in fact, from the previous Web, that we'll call Web 1.0? What has dramatically changed is the web surfers' behavior; It is no longer passive and content receiving entities, but rather active agents in the Web's development, thus multiplying by millions, the contributors to this new ecosystem called Web.

The new watchword now is collaboration. This allows for the creation of new organizational ways and the creation of a virtual extension of organizations and people, altering behaviors and attitudes towards the role of the Internet in our lives.

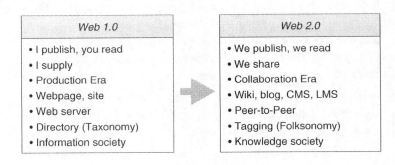

Web 1.0	Web 2.0
• I publish, you read	• We publish, we read
• I supply	• We share
• Production Era	• Collaboration Era
• Webpage, site	• Wiki, blog, CMS, LMS
• Web server	• Peer-to-Peer
• Directory (Taxonomy)	• Tagging (Folksonomy)
• Information society	• Knowledge society

Collaboration Platforms

Background

Thanks to the existence of collaboration platforms, I am writing this chapter from my hotel room, drawing inspiration from the Vistula river, running calmly in front of me.

Without collaboration platforms, I couldn't maintain my activity during travels. Since I started my computer this morning, I've already performed the following tasks:

- I used the internet from one of the organizations I work for to give my opinion on several pending situations.
- I read and added content to a work document at Google Docs.
- I exchanged messages with a Finnish colleague about a possible event in Spain.
- I gave some advice, through Facebook, to a Romanian colleague who was in Lisbon for the day, particularly about places to visit.
- I made calls, via Skype, to mobile phones and phones across Europe and I also sent some text messages.
- I downloaded the last news in terms of podcasts.

- I heard and watched news programs live, via TSF and TVI 24 (Portuguese radio and television channel, respectively).

- I tested collaboration platforms with a colleague from Cyprus.

- In other words, whether I am in my office or in a hotel in Warsaw for my contact network, – my work is equal. Personally, it is not equal; I like to change my surroundings: It inspires me!

Collaboration work is a new competence necessary for knowledge workers, allowing us to use the potential of our networks; therefore, it is important to know the tools available.

Nevertheless, we need to keep in mind that, as we will see next, we have the technology to perform a collaborative work efficiently, but the hardest part is adopting a collaboration attitude, changing our old habits that are deep within us.

. . . .

When we need to arrange a meeting, the first problem is the logistics of combining availability of spaces and schedules. We are faced with this problem every single day and we continue to live as if no solution is possible.

DimDim

There are some virtual room solutions where several people can share contents and communicate simultaneously.

DimDim is probably the most convenient solution for those who want to try this new type of meeting, because it has a free version which enables up to 20 participants per meeting, including:
- use of audio and video by participants;
- chat window;
- white board sharing;
- host's desktop sharing;
- PowerPoint presentation sharing;
- immediate registry or scheduling of a meeting.

DimDim also features paid solutions, which include more functions.

Figure 7.1. Virtual meeting rooms available at DimDim (www.dimdim.com)

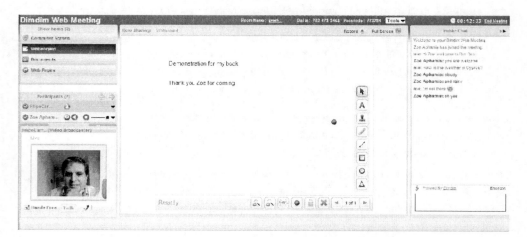

Adobe Connect

Adobe features a Flash platform to perform virtual meetings: Adobe Connect (former Macromedia Breeze) which, just as DimDim, features a free solution – Adobe Connect Now.

At the same time, Adobe also offers paid solutions that also include more functions.

Figure 7.2. Aspect of Adobe Connect Platform (www.adobe.com)

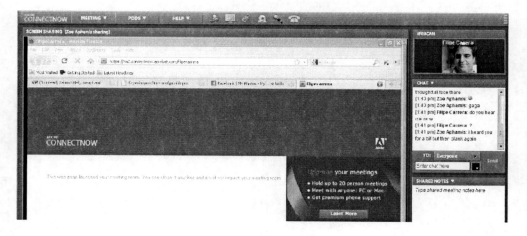

Webex is the leading and oldest platform around, created in 1995. In 2007, it was bought by the giant Cisco.

WebEx

Webex' approach is different from the competition, maybe due to market position, since it does not include a free version, except for a 14-days trial period. Nevertheless, just as the previous examples, their business model is based on monthly or annual fees.

Figure 7.3. Webex, market leader in synchronous collaborative platforms (www.webex.com)

Google Docs is an amazing tool in this day and age, since it's a major breakthrough in how we look at work documents.

And now
Google... Docs

The big issue here has appeared in multidisciplinary teams that encompass several organizations and is related to the interconnection between applications. In other words, with each company working on a particular system and with particular software, it is not possible to work in collaboration on a given document.

Google Docs is a transversal solution, which any company or individual may use, as long as there is a computer connected to the Internet. For instance, a vendor might share a document with a client, with the objective of improving a quote instead of opting for the alternative paths, such as phone calls, email exchange, meetings, etc.

With Google Docs, you can:

- Create document from scratch, such as presentations, text documents or spreadsheets.
- Create forms that can be answered online and whose results may be downloaded unto a spreadsheet, which can then be easily exported to Excel.
- Upload files to folders that can be shared later.
- Share documents safely.
- Perform online changes of shared documents.
- Organize your files into folders.

If you need a quick, easy and free solution to share and work on documents online, Google Docs will surely be the right choice.

Figure 7.4. Google Docs, a growing collaboration tool (http://docs.google.com)

Google text & tabellen

Google Docs Home

Create documents, spreadsheets and presentations online   1 of 6

Create documents,
spreadsheets and
presentations online

Share and
collaborate in real
time

Safely store and
organize your work

Control who can see
your documents

Read user examples

Get started

Create basic documents from scratch or start from a template.
You can easily do all the basics, including making bulleted lists, sorting by columns, adding tables, images, comments, formulas, changing fonts and more. And it's free.

Upload your existing files.
Google Docs accepts most popular file formats, including DOC, XLS, ODT, ODS, RTF, CSV, PPT, etc. So go ahead and upload your existing files.

Familiar desktop feel makes editing a breeze.
Just click the toolbar buttons to bold, underline, indent, change font or number format, change cell background color and so on.

With the growing importance of outsourcing and the existence of multidisciplinary project teams, it is becoming clear that the documental flux of project management and associated software programs must adapt themselves by evolving to Web platforms.

Management projects through Web platforms allow for the integration of tasks by different entities and experts, using a common interface, thus guaranteeing an immediate access to information, equal to all participants.

Another great advantage of keeping the information on a project centralized on a Web platform is allowing the access of any team member, regardless of location or the equipment used to access such information. Thus, it is possible to have a global team working on the same project.

If appropriate non-disclosure policies regarding information are followed, these platforms guarantee that no information is lost and that the changes are registered in order to allow their reversion if needed.

Project management

Figure 7.5. dotProject, an open source project management Web tool (www.dotproject.net)

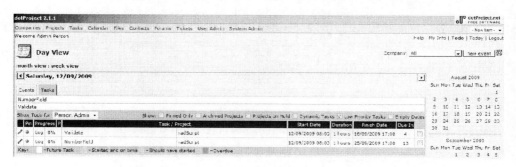

By working increasingly more in knowledge networks, where sharing resources is the new motto, and as a more ubiquitous Internet is made available, as well as more bandwidth, we will experience, less and less, the need to load our hard drives your information and associated programs.

The future lies in cloud computing which consists of sharing computer tools through system interaction, similarly to clouds in the sky, instead of having these tools on our computers.

Cloud computing

The computer will become a device that simply connects to the Internet only with input devices (keyboard, mouse, voice recognition) and output (screen and printer).

Communicating in the 21st Century

Background

Back to my trip to Mongolia I was held for 30 hours in Ulan Bator, because of weather conditions that could facilitate the landing of my flight to Beijing. I was very upset, because I had scheduled the trip back just in time to attend my youngest son's birthday party.

Despite the 8hour difference and the distance between Portugal and Mongolia, I established a video call via Skype to my son's computer, which was strategically placed in the kitchen, so that I could participate and share in the preparation of the party.

One of the most significant differences between the 20th century and the previous centuries is the extraordinary ability to communicate instantly with a contact network, regardless of locations.

Not even the Sci-fi series at the end of the 20th centuries imagined this possibility. They imagined the possibility to teletransport people, before imagining that there was no need for that.

Instant messaging services began by only offering the possibility to have a chat conversation and expanded their functions with the use of VoIP and the growing bandwidths available.

Nevertheless, I see that these new communication tools are still underused by professionals, although they have great potential where collaboration work and cost reduction are concerned.

Both organizations and individuals have access to sophisticated videoconference systems, completely free of charge, and nevertheless, they still insist on attending unnecessary meetings, that could be avoided by using these systems, thus reducing costs and executive time.

Currently, and thanks to users' status, instant messaging programs are excellent ways to inform our contact network about what's new.

On the other hand, contact networks remain cohesive, because one is made aware of the presence of our contacts, since small pop-out windows appear every time a person goes online.

Communicating with contact networks

Windows Live Messenger is the new generation of Microsoft's MSN Messenger, commonly known as MSN. This service is used by over 330 million people across the world.

MSN

Figure 7.6. MSN's aspect (http://download.live.com/messenger)

The main functions of MSN include:

- File sending.
- Folder sharing, through Windows Live SkyDrive, thus avoiding the direct transference of files.
- Chat between users.
- Audio and video communication between users.
- Calls to phones or mobile phones.
- Online games.
- Ability to use a wide range of emoticons.

Skype

Ever since Skype was launched in 2003, it became specialized in voice communication through the Internet and in 2006 it also added video communication features.

Currently, Skype's functions are quite similar to MSN's but it is more widely accepted by professionals, probably because it provides a more reliable voice and video service, as well as more developed components of calls to landline phones and mobile phones. In case of mobile phones, it even allows text messaging.

Skype also features another quite interesting characteristic; the possibility to make conference calls where a maximum of 24 people may take part simultaneously, regardless of being contacted through Skype, land phone or mobile phone.

One of Skype's latest features is the possibility of sharing desktops, thus allowing a user to see another user's desktop, which is quite handy when we're trying to explain how to do something on a computer we're not seeing.

Skype has also put great effort into trying to overcome sound quality problems during calls.

We should emphasize that, regardless of the program we use, call quality is better or worse depending mostly on the resource sharing in our computers.

For professional users who have these issues, I strongly advise you to use microphone and headsets with built-in sound cards, because you will be able to obtain a sound quality superior to that of a normal phone call.

Skype is, in fact, a program that allows us to transform our computer into a contact centre, in part thanks to the great diversity of services being offered.

Figure 7.7. Skype, a contact centre for companies and professionals (www.skype.com)

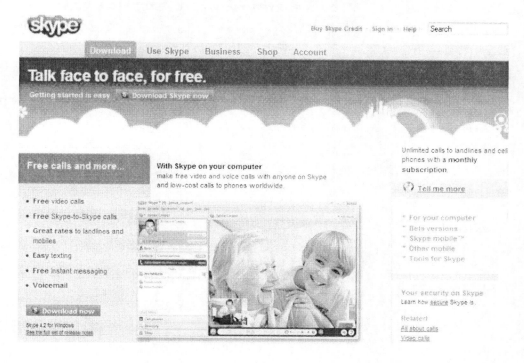

There are many other applications quite similar to VoipBuster that are Skype's main contenders since they compete on the Voice over IP market.

Free phone calls?

VoipBuster offers the possibility of performing calls to phones and mobile phones across the world in much more competitive prices than Skype and, in some cases, the calls might even be free of charge: for instance, when the destination number belongs to the Portuguese, North-American or most European landline phone networks (by the way, calls for USA's mobile phone numbers are also free!).

Text messages also have very competitive prices.

Skype's sound quality during calls is steadier and this service requires the use of microphone and headset with a built-in sound card.

Figure 7.8. An inexpensive VoIP international communication service (www.voipbuster.com)

Other alternatives	Within instant messaging and VoIP communications, the available range is not limited to Skype, MSN and VoipBuster. There are plenty of other options, such as Yahoo Messenger and Google Talk, which share the same features.
	In both cases, there is the possibility to access these services directly in the webmail access pages, a very useful function to contour the banning policies several companies have towards instant messaging services.

Figure 7.9. (http://messenger.yahoo.com and www.google.com/talk)

Within a certain measure, banning policies regarding certain websites and services have created a niche for other contents and service providers; so banning policies will always be sort of a cat and mouse play.

In my opinion, people must be responsible and made responsible for the use of the means at their disposal and their assessment should be performed regarding achieved results. This is the only way to in-

Are bans worth it?

corporate this means of communication into companies' daily work routine, stepping out of playful clandestinity.

I also believe that, in time, these bans will be eliminated; similar to what has happened with bans regarding phones, only that in this particular case the time and money lost by not using it is much more significant.

THE NETWORKER TALKS

A Global Challenge

I was at the beach discussing this book with my wife when she had the most brilliant idea: Ask my contacts who are a part of social networks to send their testimonials on how networking has affected their lives, both personally and professionally.

I prepared a message on my Facebook and LinkedIn networks, inviting them to write a small testimonial on their personal networking experiences. On Facebook, I actually created an event, which went on until the final date to receive the statements.

I made the same request through my Facebook, LinkedIn, Twitter and Plaxo statuses. Later, I placed a video, across these networks, using Seesmic and Facebook, where I explained exactly what I wanted with the testimonials.

Although it was the middle of August and a lot of people were on vacations across the entire world, and despite the short notice, I got 31 testimonials, from 18 countries.

You will see that plenty of testimonials are related to JCI (Junior Chamber International), because networking is one of the opportunity areas of this organization and its members are the main beneficiaries and, therefore, excellent networkers.

After I received and selected the testimonials, I decided to divide them into groups according to impact areas, so that one could more easily see the benefits obtained by networking activities:
• Being professionally successful.
• Having more business.
• Accessing more knowledge.
• More opportunities.
• Expanding contact networks.
• Online social networks.
• Personal development.

I also decided that I wanted to clearly identify the author, indicating name, country of origin and profile address within a social network or personal website.

Being a Successful Professional

Dealing with the crisis

As a management consultant, I work in a market which is quite sensitive to economic situations. During the 2003 Internet crisis, I was hit and had to struggle hard to get a new job.

I discovered my network to be truly insufficient. I saw no other way than reacting to open vacancies, not the best method in a difficult job market. For me, this was a valuable learning experience and I promised myself: «Never again».

Since then, I have put much effort into building and maintaining a valuable network. According to my vision, networking is about offering help and being truly interested in each other, rather than just approaching people when you need them. I soon learned to enjoy getting to know new people; my fear of networking is over, and I can't understand any more why this networking-fear was there in the first place.

I use many community sites to maintain my network and I am always updated on what is happening with whom. LinkedIn and Facebook are the ones I use the most.

Now when the financial crisis struck, my employer and I needed to find a new job again, I was amazed how easy it was to harvest my network: Just one status update on LinkedIn and ten persons immediately approached me. Even people I had not seen for over ten years approached me to 'come and have a talk'. Within a month I found the company that soon proved to be the best match; they didn't have a vacancy, but they created one for me. What more could I wish for from a well maintained network?

Patrick van der Spank, The Netherlands
www.linkedin.com/in/pvdspank

Getting to know
the other person

I joined JCI In April 2008, as I was being invited by a friend to help him develop a local project here at JCI Bucharest. The project went really well, covered 6 major cities in Romania and created a huge awareness about JCI.

Later on that year, in October, I met Tudor Maxim, who came up with the idea about Tineri Antreprenori (Young Entrepreneurs), a mentoring program that involved several well known and respected entrepreneurs from Romania becoming mentors of young and talented entrepreneurs.

Organizing this project with Tudor meant spending many nights at the office, followed by hours in pubs, relaxing after the hard work :). This eventually led to a close friendship, which later was transformed into the foundation of our business partnership. In December we began talking about developing the ideal digital marketing agency :).

So, in May 2009, while planning the second edition of Tineri Antreprenori, the idea that Tudor and I should start a new company grew even stronger. So I decided that it was for the best for me to leave the company, where I occupied the position of senior web developer, because we both wanted to create Good Afternoon!, a real digital marketing agency focused on optimal usage of digital media.

It took us over 7 months to get to know each other, and during this time, I got to discover my partner's managing and strategist qualities and he got to be aware of my creative solutions and technical knowledge. Networking does not happen overnight; it is a living process than involves trust, patience and transparency.

Mihai Nasaudean, Romania
www.linkedin.com/in/mihainasaudean

. . . .

Fresh out of my degree course, I was responsible for a Junior Company – JuniFEUP and AlumniLEIC (students' organization).

When I left JuniFEUP, I began to work at Optimus as Project Manager in the Commercial Development Department.

During my stay at Optimus, I was invited to be a speaker in a conference at FEUP, organized by JuniFEUP. During that conference, I met someone who, six months later, invited me to take over the Business Developer position at Segula Technologies Portugal.

A colleague of mine from Segula, who had left shortly after I had entered the company, ended up by recommending me for an opening at Hays, as a Recruitment Consultant.

We are constantly being watched

When I wanted to return to Porto, I was recommended by an ex-university colleague, member of AlumniLEIC, as Support Architect at Qimonda Portugal.

These leaps were caused by the contacts I developed throughout my university, association and professional career.

The attitude I have in and outside my work place allow me to develop good relationships with people. I believe that good networking in a good network is essential in this day and age.

Eduardo Espinheira, Portugal
www.linkedin.com/in/eespinheira

Communicating
our goals

I have fairly big network all around the world. I like to help everyone as much I can. It is not a shame to ask for help when we do need it; we only have to consider the possibility that they may say NO as well. There are 5 kinds of answers I usually get when I ask for help:

1. Of course and solution
2. Of course and no solution
3. Excuses
4. No answer
5. How much do you pay?

I prefer the first one.

I found my job and my house thanks to my network. It was 1993 when I got back (after a divorce and after living for 7 years in the small island of Hiiumaa).

I had nothing except for my little 5-year old son, two hands, brains and looks.

Most of my ex classmates worked and lived in Tallinn. I started to work in a small food shop and to live with my parents. I started to build up my network in Tallinn, in order to get a better job and a home.

Half a year later, I was working at a big shop and a year after I became the branch manager for the second biggest Estonian bank – Union Bank (now SEB).

I asked a client who was in real estate if I could get some extra work and I managed to buy with a very good price a nice flat, because I was collaborating with him.

Even before writing the application to the city government to get the flat, I found out that within the nice but very sad area of Pelgulinn, a lot of houses and flats were vacant and deteriorated.

I started to communicate with a local government department and discuss ways through which I could buy some of these flats and renovate them. Also as a freelancer, I wrote stories for children and other articles for the local newspaper.

I eventually managed to obtain a great network, trough which I found out that I could buy a house at an extremely good price. So 2 years after I went back to Tallinn with empty hands, I had a good job and house with a little garden.

There were enough people who thought that I had probably slept with a lot of managers (all men), since I am an interesting and attractive woman, but NO, I only used my skills to communicate to build and manage my network.

Katrin Aedma, Estonia
www.KaKonsultatsioonid.ee

The importance of contact networks

Although I have a long road ahead (I'm only 25), the masters have always tried to imprint in me the importance of a vast and faithful contact network.

These are neither friendships nor comradeships, but rather exchanges of experiences, to learn from other people's experiences and to form useful knowledge for future personal experiences (from commercial experiences to the quest for a professional path).

Recently, I changed from an Intermediary Management position to a Business Developer post. This change only took place because of the contacts established that allowed me to grab on to this new challenge.

Bearing in mind that in this line of work a good contact network is essential to succeed. I'm already doing my homework, trying to find out what are the best contacts to expand and to open «commercial» doors.

In less than a month, I have used my contact network for two specific purposes and I'm succeeding in both motivations.

Luck? Let's just say that contact networks (networking) are worked on and the way we approach the networking will determine our success, both the network's and ours!

Miguel Paixão, Portugal
www.linkedin.com/in/mpaixao

Getting More Business

A golden «hello»

On November of 2007, I was invited to a networking meeting of foreign professionals in Istanbul. The friend who invited me to the event called at the last minute and apologized because she wouldn't be able to participate. I had two options:

wait for the next time;

Test my networking skills at a «Nobody Knows Me» evening.

I chose to network! I walked into the room, I quickly looked for a familiar face. No luck! I realized I was a little nervous, so I motivated myself to feel like the host of the event and to find a smiling face that I could share a warm «Hello» with – and start networking.

I took a deep breath, caught a glimpse of the first smile and I said «Hello». This lady was working for the management of an airline company in Istanbul. For the rest of evening, I met some more new professionals via her kind introductions.

Since November 2007, I've kept in touch with her by either sending a greeting note during holidays or by sharing an interesting article on airline companies.

In 2008, I changed my job: I stopped being a consultant and started to work in a family-owned company dedicated to decoration and design. A few months ago, we decided to target not only retail business but also corporate projects such as VIP Lounges.

Sure enough I called, since we had a good relationship. I directly asked her if we could cooperate in the decoration of her airline company's lounge projects.

Well... the story, which started with a simple decision to network continued with a sincere «hello» and continuous networking over some time, resulted in a project worth more than 200 thousand Euros for my company.

Ertugrul Belen, Turkey
www.linkedin.com/pub/ertugrul-belen/2/583/331

Through the wonderful network of JCI, I met several people from the association in the border triangle of Germany, Switzerland and France. We have made some projects together to get to know how to work together and we had a lot of fun during the conferences and trainings.

One day in the summer, I got a phone call from abroad and I wondered about the number on the display.

A JCI friend told me about a problem he was having trying to buy an American company of a certain industry with activities all over the world. He needed detailed market analysis, along with figures and also some special trend analysis about the German, Austrian and some other markets.

He asked me if I knew someone who could do that difficult task. I just had to say «Yes».

It was me, and of course I quickly helped him, because we already knew each other. After our analysis he could start his negotiations and definitely decide towards the merger and, up to now, he is quite satisfied with his analysis-based decision...

Ulrich Wiener, Germany
www.linkedin.com/pub/ulrich-wiener/11/30/873

Business comes to you

Networking played a big part in my plans to organize, promote and run overseas seminars without spending a single Euro.

I'm regularly introduced by the BBC as the Marketing Magician. I took up the challenge to market without a budget because so many businesses think that marketing is always expensive and I wanted to prove this was not true.

And now penniless...

These planned seminars were to be in Portugal where I had no business contacts. I started by sending out media releases via email and news distribution sites, promoted the seminars on my website, used my regular e-newsletter and used e-networking via business/social networking sites to obtain recommendations, free coverage on radio and in a local newspaper and venue sponsorship at a local hotel. Fifty people turned up to the seminars and I now write a regular column in the local paper, write their business E-newsletter and, as an aside, was interviewed by the BBC whilst still in Portugal.

Due to combining networking with some simple free marketing ideas I was able to deliver some well received seminars in a foreign country without spending any money whatsoever. The events were so successful they are now being repeated on a regular basis.

Stefan Drew, United Kingdom
www.StefanDrew.com

Stepping out of your comfort zone

This story starts at an underground platform next to my home. I had 8 minutes until the subway arrived at downtown and I decided to start a conversation with a person who was also waiting for the train. I think I asked him how his professional life was going and he told me that he is studying at the Stockholm School of Entrepreneurship and working at a telecom-company.

He is doing a project about water-treatment in Africa (where he's originally from, Ethiopia). My absolute favorite topics are water and entrepreneurship.

Kaled and I exchanged business cards and had some meetings. He even became a member of Junior Chamber Stockholm. Today, we have started a company in Sweden and another in Ethiopia and are travelling around, doing business in West-Africa.

Today we keep each other posted through LinkedIn and e-mail. What was started by a word is nowadays a friendship!

Peter Pimpim Petterson, Sweden
www.linkedin.com/myprofile?trk=hb_side_pro

Networking is one of the most powerful selling tools, no question about it. Within a company such as Re/MAX, teaching the basic concepts of this 21st century discipline is our daily work. Our agents have a well organized contact network to increase reference and, consequently, their revenue.

My experience as a real estate agent was full of networking successes, but when the challenge came to lead the franchising expansion to RE/MAX, I had to reinvent my prospecting techniques.

I started my adventure as an expansion director on October 2008, after the collapse of Wall Street and when a deep crisis, which had settled across all industries of world economy, began to be felt by everyone.

My objective was to ensure the growth of RE/MAX network with the opening of new and successful real estate agencies. As you can imagine, from day one at my new job, there was no one available to go into the real estate industry at that time.

Our usual way of generating contacts through our website was DEAD. And, for me, it became clear that the company's administration would not take crisis as an excuse for not achieving goals. Instead of waiting for customers to knock at our door, or in another words at our email address, we decided to attack a new target: Traditional real estate agencies that do not operate within a franchising network. But how exactly would we do this? Phone calls? Emails? Fax? Door to door visits?

My first bet was simple, since we manage a network of 220 real estate agencies that are free to share businesses with any other agencies, RE/MAX affiliated or not, – why not just talk with them and see who's interested?

During my first visit to an agency, our agent mentioned an agency that was Lousada's market leader, where we needed to open an agency.

Furthermore, he confirmed that these people had great work methods and excellent service quality. The following day I was in Lousada talking to the agency's owner and, in December, they integrated our network. Thus, I signed my first franchising contract.

Today, our expansion strategy is based on networking, we have bonuses for agencies indicating potential clients, we're always present in all online networks. During the year that most considered to be a

Going beyond
the crisis

year of profound crisis in Portugal, we already managed to sign 20 new agency contracts and 2009 still isn't over.

Joanna Koltan Carvalho, Portugal
www.linkedin.com/in/joannacarvalho

Accessing More Knowledge

Knowledge communities	In our country (Lithuania), one of the largest virtual communities is www.supermama.lt. Originally, about 3 years ago, it was only a community for parents (naturally, since eventually most of us become parents sooner or later). Now it is a community that has knowledge and answers to almost all possible questions about life. Now, when Lithuanians search for something in Google (in Lithuanian), very often it starts offering answers taken from the supermama.lt forum!

I can't even count how many times I was advised by this community. For sure it helped me to select a doctor to deliver two children. Then I used it to get food recipes... then to select my own diet... then a place for family vacations... then in the choice of a house cleaning company. Even when I was selecting my laptop, the search engine offered me advice from supermama.lt!

Aurejila Muzaite-Zavanelli, Lithuania
www.linkedin.com/pub/aurelija-muzaite-zavanelli/2/324/268

The quest for knowledge	My story is simple: Besides my mission as a college teacher, I have a close link to the business world, particularly marketing management and since I am a part of several types of social networks, contacts appear.

From former students to students of organizations, everyone seems to contact me with doubts regarding scholastic issues, talent recruitment, events or other type of invitations.

This is my network and I'm proud to use it to help me and others in this eternal search for knowledge. I applied a very simple rule: I don't bother my contacts with side issues.

I try to be effective and achieve my goals. Honestly, I think that today this is the best way to make excellent businesses but be careful: we must take care of our network and be true to ourselves.

Carla Viana, Portugal
www.linkedin.com/pub/carla-viana/5/245/164

To see the power of connections and what it means to build strong long term relationships, I want to share this story with you.

Passion is attractive

When I was an English teacher, I met a lady who was working at the American Embassy in Bucharest. She later went on to Washington to occupy another position as a diplomat.

In 2003 and because I was starting my PhD in nonverbal communication, I wanted to translate the only dictionary available about this subject. It is about «The Nonverbal Dictionary of Gestures, Signs & Body Language Cues» written by Dr. David Givens.

Knowing that my friend lived in Washington, I asked her to buy this dictionary for me. She looked for it in every major book store, but she couldn't find it, so she called the author, who said that the dictionary is only available online but that he would be very pleased to advise and to share his knowledge with me.

So I wrote an email to the author and started to collaborate with him. After one month, I received an email from a friend of David Givens, Joe Navarro, a former FBI agent and teacher at the FBI Academy, who also wanted to collaborate.

It's been almost six years since I've started my professional collaboration with these two important authors on the nonverbal communication domain, which gave a lot of significance to my personal career and work.

Plus, I had the honor to translate Joe Navarro's book «What Everybody is Saying: the Guide of an ex-FBI Agent to Speed Reading People» and to organize a great business conference, featuring him as a guest in Bucharest in 2009.

This way, you can see how easy it is to start relations with famous and important people just because you are passionate about a subject and you want to do something with your life.

Mihaela Liliana Stroe, Romania
www.linkedin.com/in/mihaelalilianastroe

Sharing knowledge through a blog	Networking is useful to provide burn patients with information about medical treatment.

Some patients have come to see me from other prefectures, taking much time and travel expenses, though there are hospitals near them.

Burn patients, whose condition is not serious enough to require ambulance transportation, search online for hospitals. A Japanese website about New Wound Treatments (www.wound-treatment.jp) includes a list of all doctors in Japan who are performing the treatment named wet-dressing therapy.

I registered the website and I can provide burn patients with treatment through my blog at http://shinsatsu.exblog.jp.

There are patients who search my website for burn treatment, especially children and women.

I'm happy to treat and cure them in a shorter time span, with less pain, with less conspicuous scars, with wet-dressing therapy. Networks of doctors and my blog have helped a great deal during the treatment.

Hitoshi Fukuyama, Japan
www.linkedin.com/in/hitoshi

Social networks and knowledge sharing	When I attended the 21st JCI Academy that took place in Tachikawa, Japan, from July 11 to 18, 2008, I was serving as the 2008 JCI Lebanon Secretary General. During the Academy, I went out of my way to network and mingle with the largest number of international delegates possible, as more than half of them would be the 2009 National Presidents of their respective JCI National Organizations.

Because of that networking, I am in touch with most of them this year as the 2009 JCI Lebanon National President.

Through chats and conversations on Facebook and Skype, in addition to email exchanges, we continuously share best practices and projects that we are working on to widen our horizons and take our National Organizations to new heights.

Rania Haddad, Lebanon
www.linkedin.com/pub/rania-haddad/2/436/a01

More Opportunities

During the JCI Baltic Conference in Lithuania I accidentally met the current president of JCI Norway. We had a casual conversation and I also told him about a dream I have – travelling around the world and giving creativity trainings for young leaders. He seemed interested in that dream.

The power of dreams

A couple of months later, I participated at JCI Public Speaking Championship in Budapest and gave a good speech. A month after that, I received an e-mail from Thomas saying: «I cannot forget some of the things we talked about, and when I saw you on the stage, during the speaking competition, I was sure; I want you to come to Norway and do training for us.»

Two weeks ago, I did the training in Norway. It was great and my training tour has officially started now.

The moral is – whatever the value you are offering during networking, prove it. But most importantly – networking is about telling what yours dreams are, about your vision and about enabling others to help you achieving that dream.

Harald Lepisk, Estonia
www.linkedin.com/in/haraldlepisk

Opening doors

This is a real life experience. Hence, it is a very good example of how important a role personal networks play in a person's life. I'm an Assistant Professor of Management at Akdeniz University, Business Administration Department, Antalya. I completed my master and doctoral studies at the same university. My doctoral thesis was about managerial decision making behavior and it involved a comparison of Turkish and Japanese managers' decision making behaviors.

During my university years, I had attended a Turkish-Japanese Student Conference. This way, I began to be interested in the Japanese culture and language.

When I came back to my hometown in Antalya after graduation, the first thing I did was to become a member of Turkish Japanese Friendship Association. There we came together and shared various activities with Japanese lecturers working in Akdeniz University and Japanese people living in Antalya.

During my doctoral research, when I was faced by the problem of accessing Japanese managers working in Turkey, I talked about that to one of the Japanese lecturers who was a friend of mine from the Turkish Japanese Friendship Association. What is unbelievable is that one of his best friends was the general manager of Mitsubishi Corporation Turkey and so a contact was established. My friend let him to know me and my studies.

This way I was able to get an interview appointment, which perhaps wouldn't be accessible to an ordinary person. Through that interview, a very important door was opened on my way to do research as a part of my doctoral thesis.

Networking is Building Your Life!

Nuray Atsan, Turkey
www.linkedin.com/pun/nuray-atsan/a/236/3bb

The network's value

I've always considered myself to be the Guerrilla marketing type of entrepreneur. As a small business owner in the field of training & consulting, I am swimming in a sea with a lot of big fish. The market is very competitive and to generate clients you need to be «out there». Since I cannot take Advertising and big promotions into considerations, due to budget limitations, I've been using the power of networking to make my business grow.

For me this is the most cost-effective way to do so, and sometimes it also gives me the opportunity to be an active citizen. Some examples are:

- Joining JCI, and being active in high profile projects; This gives me the opportunity to network, not only with members but also with business and government leaders;
- Joining professional networks, business clubs, etc.

Up till now, most of my clients are from these networks. And that's just great, as I have my hands full with them. But since the power of networking is not only in getting the benefits, but also giving benefits to others, I make sure I always do that;

People from my network always receive special offers, discounted prices and even special gifts. Something I often do is inviting my (new) people in my network to register for the «Insights of the Day program». If they do, they get daily motivational messages, with my signature below. For me this is a great way to keep in touch with my network, share something nice with them every day, and of course, making sure they don't forget me...

One thing I always do is sharing my successes with everyone in my network, either by sending them the story by email or by inviting them to my blog (www.marcianolieayoung.com)

For me networking is not just about going to events, having nice chats and collecting business cards. Networking is about sharing information, being attentive, and dropping a note now and then, just to wish someone a good day.

If you network like this, people will appreciate you and if they do, getting business when the opportunity arises is a logical next step. In that way your network leads you to more net worth.

Marciano S. Lie A. Young, Suriname
www.marcianolieayoung.com

I believe in 'Doing Business Richly': doing business that feels like it has to be on my 'path' in my life. This fits exactly into my personal talents and even into my destiny in life.

Everybody wins

I have experienced that when I do business like this, one chance after another pops up, and I am doing business richly. Richly because my business generates revenue quite easily. And because it gives me a very deep feeling of satisfaction. So it makes me both economically and personally rich. And guess what happens with networking? When I do business richly, networking happens in a natural flow and with better results. Why is that?

When I do business richly and I am on my path:

• I am automatically alert and intuitively feel which persons are 'meant to be met';

• I am just authentic and we can easily make true contact;

• The true contact smoothly goes further, opportunities pop up;

• We bring opportunities into practice, generating energy;

• The outcome is even better than what I had initially imagined.

My story is true: It is my dream to bring the «Doing Business Richly» concept into the world. I was invited to conduct this training in India. I was also invited to conduct CSR in India, together with a trainer from the Cameroon. We immediately had a click, true contact. We kept in touch. He invited me to conduct «Doing Business Richly» and some networking activities in the Cameroon. I was very pleased to do that, so I went to Cameroon. The trip fully met my expectations. But then something happened I could never have imagined before.

Someone knocked at my hotel door in the Cameroon. He presented himself as the 2010 JCI World President! His appearance immediately made an impression on me. I knew: this man has to speak at a Dutch congress I was organizing.

This is what I've wanted to explain to you: while doing business richly, new valuable contacts suddenly cross your path, even if totally unexpected.

Désirée Murk-Scholten, The Netherlands
www.linkedin.com/in/desireemurk

Expanding Contact Networks

I belong to a fun little community called «Floort» (www.floort.com). Floort is a micro blog community. It is similar to Twitter except that one can comment on one another's entries and generate a long – and sometimes quite heated – conversation.

Out-of-the-box thinking

What is particularly fun about Floort is that no topic is «taboo». We talk about politics. We discuss religion. We go on and on about whether Obama is or is not a good president. Nothing is off limits. It's a paradise for those who are both opinionated and open to reading totally different ideas. I love it.

Unlike many social networking sites, however, Floort does not make it easy for people to meet and greet on a personal level. Many of us use pseudonyms and personal emails are not made available. Sometimes, though, we cheat.

I found a great friend through floort – a nurse from a nearby state called Cindy. Cindy and I exchanged personal emails through the discussion and scheduled a real meeting. It was tremendously fun to put a face to a name I had seen so many times.

Here's one last thing I love about floort – it's not about work. The networking that occurs in there is not really netWORKING – it's netLEARNING, netHAVINGFUN.

Not a single person in Floort is likely to offer me a job or purchase my services or care a button about what I do or do not for a living. It's delightfully useless from a business perspective and wonderfully energizing for my free time.

Cris Wildermuth, USA
www.linkedin.com/in/criswilsermuth

One of the most amazing success stories of our time is linkedin.com, which boosts a professional population of hundreds of millions by building networks of relationships.

What is networking?

This tendency to build networks of relationships may be genetically wired into us. It is an essential part of our survival equipment and those who do it best are often the ones who flourish in all areas of living.

Look in your life at how much of what you enjoy has been influenced by your network of relationships. Is your radio tuned to WII FM (What's In It For Me)?

Many people think of NETWORKING (building networks of relationships) as a means to solving their problems and achieving their dreams. I see problems and dreams as the occasion and impetus to connect with expanding circles of other people.

Satish Shah, India
www.linkedin.com/in/satish60449

The networks of networks

Two years ago I moved back to Finland with my new job after a 5 year break in Turkey. This meant that I had almost no network I could rely on back in Finland as most of friends and colleagues who happened to be mostly foreigners had moved out of Finland as well during the time.

I knew at that point that I needed to connect to some people in Finland at least to be able to socialize. Having been an active member of JCI in Istanbul, Turkey, I decided to contact JCI Finland National President and ask him whether there was any international chapter that I could get in touch with and start participating in the events of JCI Finland.

He suggested me to get in touch with the Immediate Past President of a chapter called the Central Park that had some other foreign members. So I did. And very soon I was already participating JCI events and had friends to call and enjoy the company of.

I believe one should look at networking not only as an opportunity-creator but also as a torch-light for people like me who can be considered as part of newly forming supranational global society.

Pinar Köse Kulacz, Finland
www.linkedin.com/in/pinarkosekulacz

Online Social Networks

Online,
we achieve more

In 2004, I lost 70 kilos. I went from weighing 151 to 81 kilos. I've managed to maintain my shape ever since.

In November 2008, I created www.powerofchange.net, a social online community (NING) to help people evolve in their lives.

Today, we are more than 2700 people who, on a daily basis, encourage and support each other to overcome challenges.

In this social network, everyone is a leader in different life changes, thus contributing with their personal experiences.

This non-profit network has grown and today people who didn't know each other are organizing meetings and activities across the country, both online and offline.

Tiago Silvério Marques, Portugal
www.linkedin.com/in/tiagosilveriomarques

If you don't have a
network, start one!

My name is Pastor Hans-Georg Peitl from the «Familie Gottes» (the family of god)-church in Vienna.

My whole life I sought for a church which would accept all other Christians, Muslim, Jewish and humanist people, under one common point: Love God, who had made all and the next, also your enemies, like Himself. In the end, I was left surrounded by churches, because what I have found was a new kind of fascism.

Then I found Facebook and I founded a group under the name CHEF-PARTIE, which believes in the following points:

1. We accept that God is the only chief of the world; however he is called: Jachwe, God, Jehova, Allah, or Builder of the universe.

2. We accept that everyone makes mistakes and so we need a Messiah: Jesus.

In 4 weeks, 500 Bishops, Pastors, Elders, Priests and Evangelists, also Jewish, Muslims and Humanists people across the world accepted these rules and came to our group, so we could start organizing the «1st International Congress of Evangelism», with members from all 5 continents, on May 2010, and also our television service www.unzensuriert.schluss.tv.

At last 10 Bishops accepted to start the «Familie Gottes» (the Family of God), a new international, Pentecostal, all-accepting, Christian church.

Hans-Georg Peitl, Austria
www.unzensuriert.schluss.tv

Obtaining contacts through Facebook videos

I mostly use Facebook as a way to store my business contacts and friends while posting basic information about me as an attorney and professional speaker. Sometimes, I post photos or an announcement, but I am definitely not one of those people who constantly post status updates. About a month ago, however, I posted a video of me giving a key note speech at a national conference for court managers in Boston.

A few comments from some of my friends were expected, but I was truly amazed at the number of people that did not know about my other career as a professional speaker. Within two weeks, quite a bit of interest was stirred up among my 500 Facebook friends and the video even lead to two offers to be a key note presenter in Iowa and in the West Indies.

Even some of my close friends told me that they knew I did some training in JCI, but had no idea that I was doing this professionally. So, I learned very quickly that a video simply posted on a social networking site can have huge returns with no marketing cost (beyond producing the video initially).

Facebook might be a fun website, but the business possibilities are endless.

Patrick W. Knight, USA
www.knightvisionseminars.com

The importance of informing your network

As I am a trainer, I happen to be in many different locations with opportunities of networking. But what is important is not meeting many new people and exchanging business cards... Keeping the contacts and using your network actively is what matters...

Recently online tools became very helpful to manage one's networks actively and I prefer Facebook as its very user friendly and fast paced.

I joined JCI 11 years ago, when I was at New York, then I moved back to Istanbul, but my JCI friends from Philippine New York Chapter are still in my Facebook profile.

This summer, I went to NYC and that was my first day in Manhattan, before I contacted any friends about my arrival... I just wrote to my status on Facebook: `Walking on the 5th Avenue` ... 30 minutes later, I received an invitation to join the meeting of JCI members that evening.

I would have missed the date if I hadn't updated my status to my friends at Facebook... Of course, I joined them that evening and jump started my days in New York with old and new friends, thanks to networking...

This first day gathering gave me more opportunities for networking and expanded my network and filled my next days with more activities that emerged from this...

Deniz Senelt, Turkey
www.linkedin.com/pub/deniz-senelt/0/2a0/761

I have travelled to the most interesting and diverse JCI conferences: Still, I lost contact with most of the JCs I met, no matter how interesting or promising they were.

I was also invited to stay at some JCI members' houses during my trips, regardless of being JCI oriented or just private. This experience taught me that JCs share more than just the same interests in social, economic and business progress: We share the same values!

I found it was time to create a platform to bring all of us together, sharing more than just business and following these principles:

- Reinforce the contacts between older JCI members
- Facilitate international locations of JCI members
- Making trips more interesting to JCI members who share their knowledge of places
- Helping to create ties between businesses within the JCI members' network (younger and older).

Being a hub
in our network

JCI Livemap Community helped me re-connect with JCI members, but it also helped me connect with JCI members I had never met before. Now I know over a dozen new JCs who are interesting to me and my business.

Although the JCI Livemap Community is already working, new features and ways for JCs to tell their personal stories are in process. I want to increase the number of JCI members worldwide, members that interact as individuals, right here at this platform and most authentically.

If you get to know a JCI through his own words and his own opinions, you get to know who you really NEED to know! And that is what it is all about.

Roy Popiolek, Germany
www.linkedin.com/in/roypopiolek

Working with Linkedin

I am currently looking for new career opportunities and also applying for a PhD. Because of my position at this moment, I decided to utilize networking and I started my connections through LinkedIn.

Since I've already worked in several industries (Automobile, Pharmaceutical, Energy and Mass Consumption) I decided to gather my contact lists, email addresses and business cards in a single database. Then I started to see that the majority of my contacts were featured on LinkedIn, even the international contacts which would be harder to recover And, in under a month, I managed to obtain 287 connections on my profile!

This has been quite useful since I recovered contacts that I'd «lost» over 15 years ago, when I first started to work at General Motors Portugal.

In this day and age, networking is an essential practice for the exchange of ideas and experiences. I'm actually reading a book on the subject, and have listed the title in my LinkedIn's reading list: How Mass Collaboration Changes Everything.

Ana Rita Oliveira
www.linkedin.com/in/anaritaoliveira

Personal Development

I met Filipe Carrera for the first time during one of his lectures in Poland.

The first impression

We had lunch in a Portuguese restaurant in Warsaw – a wonderful time, full of funny stories about his trips around the world and yet with a gentle touch of nostalgia for his own home, his own family and, of course, Portugal.

I decided it would be nice to stay in touch and I invited Filipe to join my network on LinkedIn.

A few months later I was planning my first vacation in Portugal. All the guidebooks I had were full of practical traveler suggestions but missing the point – false prophets of tourist attractions promising «genuine» adventure.

I contacted Filipe through LinkedIn asking for advice, convinced that this man would know what travelling passion is. Filipe had just returned from Mongolia. He replied immediately; I received a complete list of accurate tips and places to see in Portugal – off the beaten track – exactly what I had in mind.

I must admit, though, that if it was not for this short personal contact at lunch few months earlier, I would not have had enough trust to accept and then follow the advice the advice I was given.

Krystyna Gottman-Narozna, Poland
www.linkedin.com/in/krystynagottmannarozna

I am a recent AIESEC Alumnus. I was President of AIESEC Egypt last year, after emerging from an anti-social personality, incapable of getting myself to walk to a microphone and speak to any audience. Nevertheless, I approached a new group of people...

Sometimes, we need to reinvent ourselves

An AIESEC Coach told me once, that you are able to re-invent yourself when you are surrounded by new surroundings/people, so you can be whoever you want to be when you enter a new room and meet new people.

Therefore, when I boarded the plane to greet 600 new people in International Congress in AIESEC, I just did that and I became the person I was always to afraid to become, and my networking helped hugely and allowed me to portray a confident and extroverted personality.

Hence, my contact network grew quickly.

Dalia Said, Egypt
www.linkedin.com/pub/dalia-said/10/3/761

Living networking

Networking is a way of life. In my life it enables me to create contacts, to potentiate my professional career, to organize my personal and social economy, to reduce time and costs.

It takes a lot of training and method; it also takes training in information, time, conflict and behavior management, as well as some learning of how to communicate.

Social networks – Facebook, LinkedIn, Twitter, Plaxo, NetLog, etc. – have immense potentials. They have been a way for me to get in touch with new people, to establish partnerships, to exchange synergies and for continuous learning.

Your screening method, according to your goals, is extremely important, because otherwise you might run the risk of losing human contact, something that is both unique and irreplaceable. For me, these tools exist to make our life easier, to speed up the first contacts and to reduce distances.

Margarida Rebelo, Portugal
www.linkedin/com/pub/margarida-rebelo/12/201/728

SIMPLIFICATION

A

AIDA

A communication model which aims to obtain **A**ttention, **I**nterest, **D**esire and **A**ction.

The objective is to write an email message or an advertisement that gets the reader's attention that motivates his /her interest for a product or a service. Something that stimulates the desire to obtain and to provoke a predetermined action.

B

Banner ad

A graphical web advertising unit, typically measuring 468 pixels wide and 60 pixels tall (i.e. 468 × 60).

BCC

Blind Carbon Copy, field used to send an email message to several people, without anyone else knowing who also received that same message.

Blog

Term derived from Web log. A site normally maintained by an individual or by a group of individuals that is updated by regular posts. These posts are presented chronologically and classified according to key-words or relevant sentences.

Bookmark

A link stored in a Web browser for future reference.

Brochureware

Current designation for a website in which the information was transferred directly into the Internet through a pre-existing paper support.

Button

A graphical advertising unit, smaller than a banner ad, usually 125 × 125, 120 × 90, 120 × 60, 88 × 31 or 120/240 pixels. When clicked, it executes a program or redirects the user to another page.

C

CC

Carbon Copy – field used to send emails to several recipients with the objective of showing everyone that all the recipients were notified.

Chat
: Communication in text and real time between two or more individuals, via computer.

Clicks
: The opportunity for a user to select a given button or link on a website and establish a connection online.

Clickstream
: A Clickstream is the recording of what a computer user clicks on while Web browsing or using another software application. As the user clicks anywhere in the webpage or application, the action is logged on a client or inside the Web server, as well as possibly the Web browser, routers, proxy servers, and ad servers.

  Clickstream analysis is useful for Web activity analysis, software testing, market research, and for analyzing employee productivity.

Click-Through
: The process of clicking through an online advertisement to the advertiser's destination.

Clipping
: Is the cutting-out of articles from a offline or online publication.

Co-creation
: Co-creation is a form of market or business strategy that emphasises the generation and ongoing realisation of mutual firm-customer value.

  It views markets as forums for firms and active customers to share, combine and renew each other's resources and capabilities to create value through new forms of interaction, service and learning mechanisms.

  It differs from the traditional active firm – passive consumer market construct of the past.

Collaborative filtering
: A program that compiles opinions of web users on a theme and makes them available for others in real time.

Contact
: An individual, within a shared social network, with whom one has confirmed to share a relationship.

Cookie
: A file registered within the computer's hard drive that uniquely identifies the user of that browser.

  There are two types of cookies: Persistent and sessions. The first ones remain on the user's computer until they are deleted or expired. Session cookies are temporary and are deleted when the browser is closed.

Crowdsourcing — The practice of using contributions from non-professionals on a task that would normally be performed by a single individual.

CTR — Click-Through Rate – The average number of click-throughs per hundred ad impressions, expressed as a percentage.

Customization — Individual adaptation of products, services and marketing messages to a particular consumer.

D

Digest — A summary of news, events or articles published in a given week or month from a given website. The summary is then sent by email to members on a mailing list.

Directory — A structured list according to categories of registered sites. It's the digital version of the yellow pages.

Domain — System of Internet addresses that consists of a sequence of names separated by dots.

E

Emoticon — A set of characters with an own meaning that intends to convey emotions associated with the text.

Emoticon	Meaning
:-)	Happiness, surprise, smile
:-D	Laughing
:'-)	Very happy
:-(	Sad
:'-(	Very sad
:-O	Astonished
;-)	Sarcastic, winking
:-Q	Smoking
8-x	Kiss

Emoticon	Meaning
8-)	With glasses
B-)	With sun glasses
:-d	Sticking the tongue out
:-{	With a moustache
:-{}	With painted lips
:-@	Screaming
P-)	Winking
:'(	Crying
>:-[	Upset
I-O	Yawning
:-I	Indifferent
:-&	Tongue-tied
O:-)	I'm a saint
:-$	Speaking of money
d:-)	With a cap
:-/	Skeptic, disbeliever
auto:-0	No screaming
@=	In favor of nuclear war
@---->---	A flower

Encrypt   Coding a message so that it cannot be read by anyone that does not have the necessary code. It is a way to provide security to emails.

E-newsletter   Email message sent to a group of web surfers with the same profile with information about a company, brand or/and product.

F

Feed   A shortened version of a Web document that presents the most recent uses.

Used in social networks to show the most recent status updates both from your profile and the profiles of the people within your social network.

Folksonomy

Also known as collaborative tagging, social classification, social indexing or social tagging.

It defines a top-down classification system, where creators of contents or the people viewing them, create tags (key-words) to classify digital contents, such as files, videos, images, etc.

The word folksonomy is a conjugation of folk and taxonomy.

Forum

Similar to newsgroups; the user can use it to submit opinions or answer messages according to themes.

G

GPS

Global Positioning System.

Groupware

Technology capable of making teamwork more productive, almost always supported by email applications, including teleconferences, group schedules, document management, digital forms and sharing of information.

H

Homepage

A website's index page, generally containing the option menu, and links to other resources within the site.

Hosting

Solution provided by an ISP for sharing contents online, normally in a shared server.

HTML

HyperText Mark-up Language – programming language to produce pages and links on the Internet.

HTML files share the .html or .htm extensions.

Hyperlink

Words or images on a webpage that, when clicked, will direct the user to another page or site.

Hypertext

Part of a text that, when clicked, will instruct the browser to search for a different page. Normally, browsers show underlined hypertext and, when an approximation is performed on the link, the cursor takes on the form of a hand.

I

IRC	Internet Relay Chat – communication tool which enables real-time text-based conversations between two or more people connected to the Internet.

K

Keyword	Indexed entry that indicates a specific file or document (key-word).

L

Link	Address connecting to a different document.

M

Mailing list	Group of people gathered around a common theme, exchanging information among them. Mailing lists may be moderated or not, just as they can be opened or closed to new subscriptions.

The difference between a mailing list and a forum lies in the fact that the participation in a mailing list is performed through email messages, whereas the participation in a forum takes place on a webpage via a reply form, supplied by the website. |
Mass customization	Use of digital technologies to adapt products, services and marketing messages to consumer groups with the same profile needs.
MDA	Mobile Digital Assistant – small device that results from fusing a PDA, a mobile phone, a GPS and a computer, which allows Internet connection through GPRD, UMTS and Wi-Fi.
Media streaming	Media streaming allows for the reading of a file, about 10 seconds after a download is begun, contrary to the majority of files that can only be read after the download is completed.

Meet-up   Online social network that facilitates face-to-face gatherings in seve-
                    ral locations across the world. Meet-ups allow their members to meet
                    and join groups according to common interests.

Microblogging   Action of sending a brief message (normally less than 140 charac-
                    ters long) to a blog or microblogging service, such as Twitter. Messa-
                    ges are instant and easily sent through mobile devices, such as cell
                    phones.

Microcelebrity   An individual that has obtained fame in a given industry or social
                    group, typically from online resources.

Moderator   Person who coordinates and moderates a mailing list or a virtual
                    community. His/her function is to establish debate themes and avoi-
                    ding possible offensive messages to be distributed to the community
                    members.

MP3   MPEG-1 Audio Layer 3, more commonly referred to as MP3, is a
                    patented digital audio encoding format using a form of lossy data
                    compression.

                    It is a common audio format for consumer audio storage, as well as a
                    de facto standard of digital audio compression for the transfer and
                    playback of music on digital audio players.

MP4   MPEG-4 Part 14 or MP4 file format, formally ISO/IEC 14496-14:2003,
                    is a multimedia container format standard specified as a part of
                    MPEG-4. It is most commonly used to store digital video and digital
                    audio streams, especially those defined by MPEG, but can also be
                    used to store other data such as subtitles and still images. Like most
                    modern container formats, MPEG-4 Part 14 allows streaming over
                    the Internet.

                    A separate hint track is used to include streaming information in the
                    file. The official filename extension for MPEG-4 Part 14 files is .mp4,
                    thus the container format is often referred to simply as MP4.

N

Netiquette   Set of rules of good behavior, non-written and non-mandatory, used
                    in communications between Internet users.

Newsgroup   Discussion group at Usenet oriented towards specific themes.

O

Offline   Term used when a person is not connected to the Internet. For ins-
                     tance, many people read email messages while offline.

Online   Term used when a person is connected to the Internet.

P

PDA   Personal Digital Assistant – mobile electronic device that works as
                     an electronic schedule and, in some cases, allows mobile phone
                     access.

Post   Message sent into a virtual community, blog, discussion group, mai-
                     ling list or discussion forum.

R

RSS   Really Simple Syndication – XML format created to share news
                     headlines and other web contents.

S

Search engine   A tool that groups pages of registered websites. Web surfers may
                     search webpages using related words with the information to be
                     obtained.

Search marketing   Action of publicizing a website through search engines, both by
                     improving the positioning within the organic research and/or by
                     buying ads on the search engines.

SEO   Search Engine Optimization – action of altering a website to grant it
                     with more visibility in search engines' organic search.

Server   Computer that shares information and resources with other compu-
                     ters also connected within a network.

Signing up — Process through which users provide certain information about themselves, in order to have exclusive access to contents from a website. This is an excellent way to build a database.

Site or website — Name given to an Internet address that aggregates a group of pages on a given subject.

SMS — Short Message Service – system that allows mobile phones to exchange text messages, with a maximum of 160 characters per message.

Social capital — It refers to the dimension of an individual's contact network and to the potential value of that network.

Social coin — Information or valuable assets that are shared with the objective of reinforcing the sense of belonging to a group that has the advantage of encouraging new social interactions.

Social media — Internet-based tools for sharing and discussing information between human beings. This term also refers to technologies that integrate technology, social interactions, photos, videos and audio.

Social network — Traditionally, this is a community in which individuals are, in some way, connected (through friendship, values, work relationships, ideas, etc.).

The modern definition of a social network including web tools, where people are connected with each other.

Social networking — Way to expand personal and professional contacts, performing connections through people.

Social trendsetter — A person with the ability to influence the actions of the other individuals within his/her social network, through his/her actions and ideas.

Spam — Marketing messages sent to a great number of people who didn't request such information.

The term spam originates from a Monty Python's sketch, in which two people in a restaurant were incapable of maintaining a normal conversation, because they were constantly being interrupted by a group of Vikings, sitting on the next table, who kept singing the Spam song.

There is a different theory stating that this term was somewhat related to the name given to canned beef in the USA.

Spam filter	Program that has the objective of blocking unsolicited emails messages.
Spammer	Every individual that sends unsolicited email messages (SPAM).
Spamming	The action of sending unsolicited email messages.
Spider	Also known as robot, it is a program developed by search engines that automatically travels through the Internet, normally to index websites' contents, registering relevant information on the databases from the respective search engines.
Sponsorship	Advertising that seeks to establish a deeper association and integration between an advertiser and a publisher, often involving coordinated beyond-the-banner placements.
Status update	One or two sentences describing your activity or thoughts, placed on a social networking website. This may include images, sounds and videos.
Sub-domain	A branch of the main domain, highly used in big websites.
Subscribe	Voluntarily signing up on a database to receive periodic updates, such as newsletters, promotions or other commercial messages.

T

Tag	Keyword to classify a digital element, such as a site, an image or a video. With this type of metadata, the element is described in order to facilitate its search.
	These tags are chosen informally by the creator or by the person visualizing the content.
Tagging	Action of creating tags. Tagging has become quite popular in Web 2.0 websites, being an indivisible from this new reality.
Thread	Term used in discussion groups that serves to define messages referring to a given theme or subject.
	Thus, threads are formed by the original message and the groups of formerly sent messages that have the objective of answering the original message.

Traffic   Quantity of data received through the Internet. It is used to refer to
                                 the number of users on a given site.

Transparency   Practice of easily making data accessible and visible to visitors on a
                                 website or blog. It can also refer to the difficulty in hiding information
                                 placed online.

Tweet   A status update sent via Twitter.

U

Unsubscribe   Just as the name says, it characterizes the action of deleting one's
                                 registry from a database.

URL   Uniform Resource Locator – text indicating a website's address.

V

Virtual community   Said when a website features functions such as forums and chats, as
                                 to promote communication among users. The advantage behind a
                                 virtual community lies on the generation of contents by the users.

Viral marketing   Online equivalent of word of mouth, sometimes referred to as a word
                                 of mouse. It occurs when several emails are repeatedly resent for fri-
                                 ends, colleagues and families.

Vlog   Short name for Video blog. A form of blog, in which the updates and
                                 comments are made through links to videos and texts.

VoIP   Voice Over Internet Protocol – term used to name the phone servi-
                                 ces over the Internet, which consists of using the web to transmit
                                 phone conversations, eliminating high costs in long distant calls.

W

Wall   Technical term for a webpage that contains spaces in which the user
                                 inputs information.

Web form	Technical term for a webpage that contains spaces where the user inputs information.
	Many of such sites have forms serving different purposes: User sign up process, shopping, commercial research, etc.
Webcam	A video camera to obtain images to use in websites.
Webdesign	Specific design for web contents.
Widget	A small software piece that fans may place on social networks' profiles, sites or blogs.
Wireless	Communication signs' transmission through antennae, similarly to those used by phone mobile providers.
WTP	Wireless Transfer Protocol – protocol to transfer information between mobile devices.
WWW	World Wide Web. It consists of a group of servers connected on a network, allowing for the exchange of information according to a unified format (html).

References

Carrera, Filipe: *Marketing Digital na Versão 2.0 – O que não pode ignorar*, Edições Sílabo, Lisboa, Portugal, 2009.

Buffini, Brian: *Work by Referral*, Buffini & Company, Inc, Carlsbad, CA, USA.

Barabási, Albert Lásló: *Linked – How Everything Is Connected to Everything Else and What it Means for Business, Science, and Everyday Life*, Plume, Massachusetts, USA, 2003.

Gitomer, Jeffrey: *O Livro Negro do Networking*, M. Books, São Paulo, Brasil, 2008.

Powell, Juliette: «33 Million People in the Room – How to Create, Influence and Run a Successful Business and Social Networking», Financial Times Press, New Jersey, USA, 2008.

Darling, Diane: *The Networking Survival Guide – Get the Success You Want by Tapping into the People You Know*, McGraw-Hill, New York, USA, 2003.

D'Souza, Steven: *Brilliant Networking – What the best networkers know, do and say*, Pearson Education Limited, Harlow, Great Britain, 2008.

Evans, Dave: *Social Media Marketing – An hour a day*, Wiley Publishing, Indianapolis, USA, 2008.